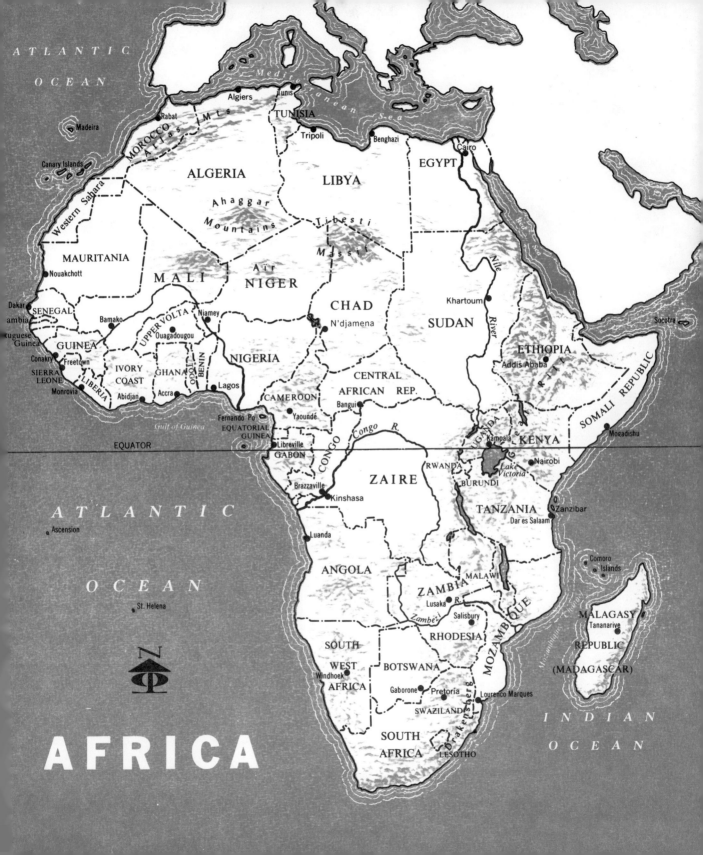

Enchantment of Africa

ALGERIA

by ALLAN CARPENTER
and TOM BALOW

Consulting Editors
Program of African Studies
Northwestern University
Evanston, Illinois

 CHILDRENS PRESS, CHICAGO

THE ENCHANTMENT OF AFRICA

Available now: Algeria, Benin (Dahomey), Botswana, Burundi, Cameroon, Central African Republic, Chad, Congo (Brazzaville), Egypt, Equatorial Guinea, The Gambia, Gabon, Ghana, Guinea, Ivory Coast, Kenya, Lesotho, Liberia, Libya, Malagasy Republic (Madagascar), Malawi, Mali, Mauritania, Morocco, Niger, Nigeria, Rhodesia, Rwanda, Senegal, Sierra Leone, Sudan, Swaziland, Tanzania, Togo, Tunisia, Uganda, Upper Volta, Zaïre Republic (Congo Kinshasa), Zambia
Planned for the future: Equatorial Guinea, Ethiopia, Somalia, South Africa

ACKNOWLEDGMENTS

Ministere de l'information et de la culture, Algiers; Service of American Interests, Ambassade Suisse dans la République Algerienne, Algiers

Cover: A typical marketplace, Allan Carpenter
Frontispiece: Bedouins from the south of Algeria graze their camels, United Nations

Project Editor: Joan Downing
Assistant Editor: Elizabeth Rhein
Manuscript Editor: Janis Fortman
Map Artist: Eugene Derdeyn

LIBRARY OF CONGRESS
CATALOGING IN PUBLICATION DATA

Carpenter, John Allan, 1917-
  Algeria.
  (Enchantment of Africa)

  SUMMARY: Introduces the history, geography, people, culture, and government of Algeria, the second largest country on the African continent.
    1. Algeria—Juvenile literature. [1. Algeria]
  I. Balow, Tom, joint author. II. Title.
  DT275.C37   965   77-20876
  ISBN 0-516-04551-2

Contents

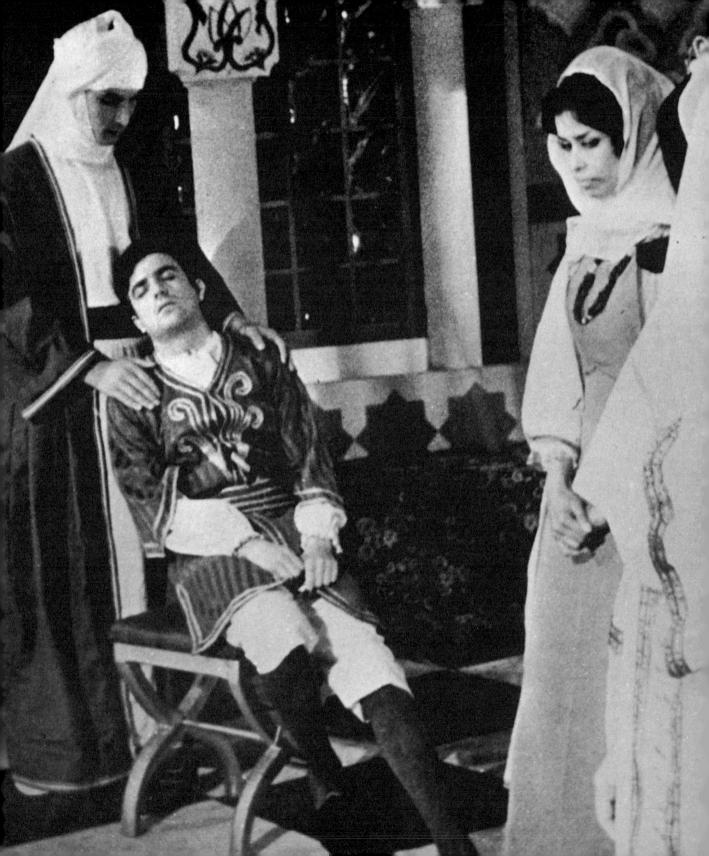

A True Story to Set the Scene

WHILE MEN WALKED THE MOON

The first performers and guests began to arrive in early July. Airplane after airplane landed at the Dar El Beida international airport, ten miles east of the city of Algiers. Between four and five thousand special visitors arrived in all, some of them wearing their native costumes. Guides and attendants transported the visitors and their baggage to hotels in this capital city of Algeria. There they rested and then began to iron costumes, polish ornaments, adjust musical instruments, and rehearse their lines and songs and dances.

The people of Algiers had spent feverish months preparing for the arrival of the visitors. Theaters had been redecorated and equipped with new lights and sound amplifiers. Outdoor stages with portable scenery had been erected in several of the city's large public squares. A special health center had been equipped with emergency medical facilities. A press center had been set up for journalists from around the world. Streets had been decorated with lights and flags and huge luminous panels.

On Monday, July 21, the detailed preparations were complete, and the gala festival began. But on that day in 1969, the attention of the rest of the world was attracted elsewhere. The speeches and performances and displays in Algiers drew little international attention. For on the first day of the First Pan-African Cultural Festival, two Americans became the first humans ever to walk on the moon.

Theatrical performances, like this one, were an important part of the First Pan-African Cultural Festival.

African artifacts, such as this lamp, were displayed in museums during the Festival.

PLANNING THE FESTIVAL

Plans for the festival had been begun several years earlier by a commission of the Organization of African Unity (OAU), a group of African nations that had achieved liberation and independence during the late 1950s and the 1960s. Thirty-

five of the forty-one independent African nations accepted invitations to the festival. Late in 1967 Algeria's proposal to act as host of the affair was accepted.

After its independence in 1962, Algeria had become a leader among the new African nations. It nationalized (put under government control) foreign-owned businesses and industries. In this way, the new nation demanded the right to benefit from its own resources. Algeria soon became a spokesman for the underdeveloped nations of the world, insisting that they obtain and keep political independence from the mighty industrialized powers that had made many of them into colonies.

It seemed only natural, then, that Algeria should play host to a demonstration of Africa's cultural heritage. Social and economic development aside, the people of the continent were discovering that their history had cultural values that had not been destroyed by foreign domination.

The festival was designed to put the life of the African people in its historical perspective, to show that their cultures had always been, and continued to be, an integral part of their lives.

TWELVE INTERNATIONAL DAYS

For twelve days the festival continued, filling the whole city of Algiers with parades, crowded streets, indoor and outdoor performances, and wildly enthusiastic receptions. As the host nation, Algeria had opened the first night of the festivities with a show of its native music and dance at the huge outdoor stadium in Algiers.

At later music-and-dance performances, tall Sudanese dancers moved rhythmically, tom-toms from Chad echoed through the stadium, Zambian ritual dancers entranced the crowd, and Nigerians demonstrated their own dances with lances and whips. Nearly every nation was represented by a traditional-dance troupe, and many nations presented modern-day ballets.

The music of myriad African musical instruments filled the streets and theaters throughout the festival. World-famous black performers from the United States showed how jazz had its roots in African music.

Besides the songs and dances, there were theatrical performances by troupes from Tunisia, Senegal, Ghana, Cameroon, and many other nations. Some of the plays told of traditional myths and legends, while others were contemporary dramas depicting various struggles for independence.

Showings of 293 motion pictures demonstrated how African filmmakers were contributing to this art form.

Museums and galleries all over Algiers were filled with displays of African painting and sculpture. Modern art was hung, and exhibitions of prehistoric artifacts and traditional handicrafts were held. Ancient manuscripts and contemporary literary works were on display.

At the lavish Palace of Nations, scholars and social scientists met for ten days to discuss the art and culture of Africa. It was agreed that the culture of a country could not develop until its people were free. Once free, the people could open up and improve their lives through their culture—as much as through technology, science, and economic development.

While humans were first walking on the moon, the festival in Algiers opened the way to a rebirth and a better understanding of the culture of Africa. While the rest of the world watched a science-fiction dream of the future come true 250,000 miles away, the festival sought its past in art and history.

Algeria's President Houari Boumediene said in a speech at the festival's opening: "What meaning, what role, what function can we assign to our culture, teaching and art, unless it is that of creating a better life for all our liberated peoples, of continuing the struggle to free our brothers still under the colonial yoke, and of thus participating in some way in the universal rehabilitation of man by man."

The better life of which President Boumediene spoke was one for which his nation had fought long and hard. Through its example, he hoped that Algeria could show the underdeveloped nations of Africa and the rest of the world how to find a better life.

Irrigation is necessary for farming in many sections of Algeria.

10

The Face of the Land

TENTH IN SIZE

Algeria lies atop the northwestern hump of Africa, extending for 620 miles along the Mediterranean Sea. It faces Spain, France, and Italy across the sea. Like the other nations of North Africa—Morocco, Tunisia, and Libya—Algeria is separated from the rest of Africa by the Sahara. And again like its North African neighbors, Algeria is not typical of the rest of the continent in climate, history, language, re-

ligion, population, and natural resources.

Its area—approximately 919,590 square miles—makes Algeria the world's tenth-largest nation in size, one-fourth as big as the United States. Only one other African nation, Sudan, is larger than Algeria. Yet Algeria ranks only forty-first among the nations of the world in population. That is because about five-sixths of Algeria is desert. Besides Sudan, five other countries on the African continent have larger populations than Algeria. Yet these countries —Ethiopia, Morocco, Nigeria, Republic of South Africa, and Zaire—are smaller in size than Algeria.

Algeria is bordered by Tunisia and Libya to the east, Niger and Mali to the south, and Morocco, Spanish Sahara, and Mauritania to the west. Some of the official boundary lines were only recently decided or are still in dispute.

The borders with Libya and Tunisia were contested in recent years when oil was discovered near the boundary lines. But these borders were finally settled in 1956 and 1970, respectively.

The Nigerian, Malian, and Mauritanian borders are mainly straight lines set out early in this century when (along with Algeria) those countries were French colonies. After Algeria became an independent nation, work proceeded on finally settling the exact path of those three borders. The border with Spanish Sahara, only twenty-six miles long, was settled in the late 1950s.

Because the Moroccan border was not specifically defined in colonial times, a dispute occurred in the 1960s over iron ore deposits in the Sahara along the border. Finally, in 1972, Algeria and Morocco signed an agreement. They allowed the disputed area to remain part of Algeria, but they set up a two-nation company to mine the ore.

THE TELL

Algeria's geography is complicated and varied. It ranges from heavily populated, humid coastal lands to dry, barren desert, where nothing lives, and from steep-cliffed mountains more than a mile high to the

MAP KEY

Ahaggar Mts., F4
Ain el Hamman, A4
Algiers, A3
Amour Mts., B3
Annaba, A5
Aures Mts., A4

Biban Mts., A4

Chelif River, A3
Chott ech Chergui, B3

Chott el Hodna, B3
Constantine, A4

Dahra Mts., A3
Djurdjura Mts., A4

El Golea, C4

Great Eastern Erg, C5
Great Western Erg, C3

Green Belt of Trees, B4

Hodna Mts., A4

Kabylia Mts., A4
Ksour Mts., C3

Mount Tahat, F4

Oran, B2
Ouled Nail Mts., B4

Quarsenis Mts., A3

Sahara Desert, G3
Saharan Atlas Mts., B3
Saoura River, C2
Seybouse River, A5
Skikda, A4
Soummam River, A4

Tafna River, B2

Tamanrasset, F4
Tanezrouft Desert, F2
Tell Atlas Mts., A3
Tipasa, A3
Tlemcen, B2
Touil River, B3
Trans-Saharan Road, D3
Traras Mts., B2

Zeralda, A3
Zab Mts., B4

12

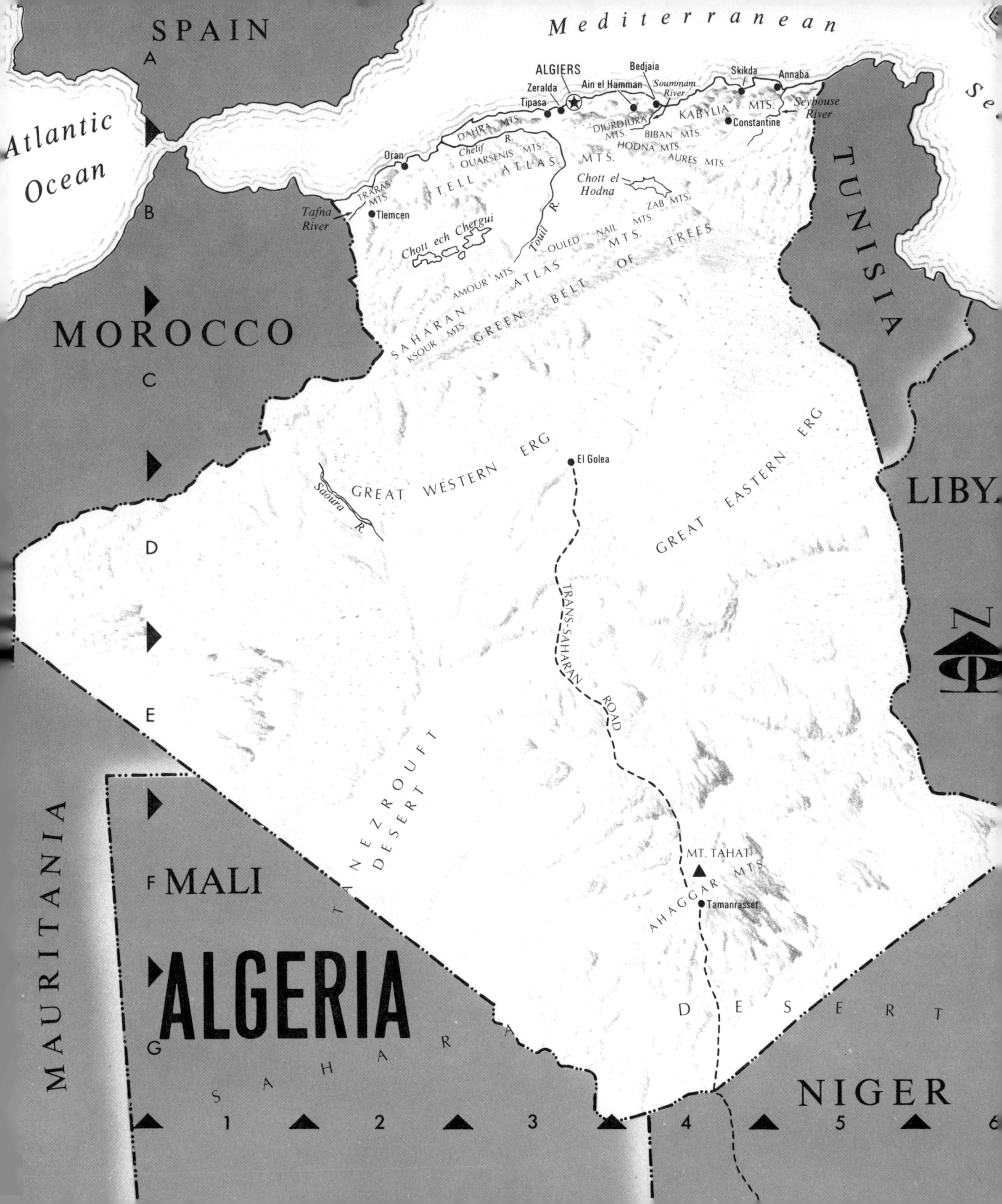

SPAIN

Mediterranean

Atlantic Ocean

ALGIERS
Zeralda
Tipasa
Ain el Hamman
Bedjaia
Soummam River
Skikda
Annaba
KABYLIA
Seybouse River
Oran
DJURDJURA MTS.
BIBAN MTS.
HODNA MTS.
Constantine
DAHRA MTS.
Chelif R.
OUARSENIS MTS.
AURES MTS.
TELL ATLAS MTS.
Chott el Hodna

MOROCCO

TRARAS MTS.
Tafna River
Tlemcen
Chott ech Chergui
Touil R.
OULED NAIL MTS.
ZAB MTS.
AMOUR MTS.
ATLAS
GREEN BELT OF TREES
SAHARAN
KSOUR MTS.

TUNISIA

LIBYA

Saoura R.
GREAT WESTERN ERG
El Golea
GREAT EASTERN ERG

TRANS-SAHARAN ROAD

N

MAURITANIA

TANEZROUFT DESERT

MT. TAHAT
AHAGGAR MTS.
Tamanrasset

MALI

ALGERIA

SAHARA

DESERT

NIGER

1   2   3   4   5   6

low, sandy beaches of the Mediterranean. Basically the country is divided into three main geographical regions by two ranges of the Atlas Mountains that cross Algeria in a general east-west direction.

The Tell Atlas Mountains lie parallel to the coast, sometimes reaching it and sometimes leaving a coastal plain two hundred miles wide. South of this coastal plain and mountainous area, known as the Tell, are high plateaus ranging from thirteen hundred to four thousand feet high, ending in another range of the Atlas Mountains known as the Saharan Atlas. And south of the high plateaus lies Algeria's portion of the Sahara.

To the west, between Algiers and the Moroccan border, the Tell is a strip of low hills, about eighty miles wide. This is Algeria's main agricultural land. The western Tell is composed of several different ranges, including the Traras Mountains near Morocco and the Dahra Mountains (about 150 miles long), between Oran and Algiers. South of the Dahra Mountains lie the Ouarsenis Mountains.

The eastern half of the Tell has a wider north-south range of hills and mountains. The Kabylia and Djurdjura Mountains along the coast average from three thousand to seventy-five hundred feet in altitude. Farther east along the coast are the lower mountains of the Kabylia. South of these coastal ranges are three connected mountain chains—the Biban, Hodna, and Aures. Some of the highest mountains are the Aures, which rise more than seventy-five hundred feet.

THE HIGH PLATEAUS

The Saharan Atlas Mountains proceed in a northeasterly direction from the easternmost tip of Morocco to the Chott el Hodna, south of the Hoda Mountains. (Chott, sometimes spelled shat, means "swampy" or "marshy area.") Generally higher (five to seven thousand feet) and less disconnected than the Tell Atlas, the Saharan Atlas consists mainly of three continuing ranges—the Ksour, the Amour, and the Ouled Nail. The Saharan Atlas stops before it reaches the Aures Mountains of the Tell. Between the two ranges are the Zab Mountains, a low ridge that makes a gap for travel between the Tell and the Sahara.

Between the Tell and Saharan Atlas mountains are Algeria's high plateaus, covering about twenty thousand square miles. These plateaus climb from a little more than one thousand feet near Chott el Hodna in the east to about four thousand feet in the west. Most of the plateaus are flat and dry with small areas of scrub and many salty marshes, the largest of which is Chott ech Chergui. The high plateaus and the Saharan Atlas are sparsely populated.

THE SAHARA

More than eight hundred thousand square miles of Algeria is covered by the Sahara, the world's largest desert. Three thousand miles wide and one thousand miles from north to south, the Sahara is

This solitary road winds through the shifting sands of the vast Sahara.

possibly the hottest, driest, and most uninviting spot on the face of the earth. Yet about half a million people live in Algeria's portion of the desert. They are either nomads who roam the northern Sahara or permanent settlers who live near the oases that dot the desert.

Only a portion of Algeria's Sahara is covered by the shifting, sun-bleached sand dunes that people often think of when visualizing a desert. There are rocky plateaus which rise above the sand, stone-covered flat regions, and even mountains, including the Ahaggar Range, which has the highest peak in Algeria—ten-thousand-foot-high Mount Tahat.

Immediately south of the Saharan Atlas Mountains are Algeria's two largest sandy deserts, the Great Western Erg and Great Eastern Erg. (An *erg* is a sandy desert.) The baking heat, blinding light, and gracefully sculptured dunes of the ergs cover about a quarter of the total area of Algeria's Sahara. From time to time, the monotony of the sand is broken by oases, with their clumps of palm trees. The wells that water the oases come from underground rivers which once flowed on the surface of the earth. A few of the oases are so large that they each provide enough water for five hundred thousand to one million palm trees.

The barren, rocky Ahaggar Mountains are in southeastern Algeria, near the Libyan and Nigerian borders. Surrounding the Ahaggar, which averages five to six thousand feet in height, are plateaus of sandstone that were once cut by rivers. As bar-

15

ren as the Ahaggar is, a few nomads live in and around it.

But to the west, along the border with Mali, is the Tanezrouft Desert, a desert not of sand but of pebbled stones. Not a blade of grass grows on the Tanezrouft. There are no oases, no one lives there, and it is said that few persons have ever crossed it.

OUED

Most of Algeria's rivers and streams are in the Tell, and they empty into the Mediterranean Sea. These *oued* (streams or rivers) flow along slowly. In the rainy season they flood, but in the summer they usually dry up completely or are reduced to feeble trickles.

The longest and largest of these is the 150-mile-long Chelif River, which for most of its course runs parallel to the coast a few miles inland. Other oued that reach the sea are the Seybouse, Soummam, and Tafna. The valleys of these oued form natural farming areas, and some of the oued have been dammed to bring irrigated water to crops.

Farther south in the Tell and in the high plateaus, the few streams that exist usually disappear under the constant hot sun or run off into salty marshes.

The Saharan Atlas Mountains have many streams coursing down their slopes. Those that flow northward into the high plateaus usually dry up before reaching the Tell. Only one of these, the Touil, crosses the plateaus and reaches the Chelif River in the wettest of rainy seasons. The streams that flow southward from the mountains are soon evaporated in the ergs of the Sahara.

Many of the oases in the Great Western and Great Eastern ergs lie above an underground river, the Saoura, which centuries ago flowed on the surface of the earth. Ancient paths of conduits (channels) are still visible and indicate where the river once ran.

In the southeastern Ahaggar Mountains are a few oued that flow when occasional rains fall. But the streams reach only short distances into the surrounding plateaus. In some of these plateaus, archaeologists have found prehistoric rock drawings of animals and plants that evidently once thrived in the area. This indicates that large rivers once coursed down the Ahaggar and that humans, animals, and vegetation once thrived at its base.

CLIMATE

Algeria's varied geography causes types of climate that are amazingly different. Along the Mediterranean coast, the wet winter season produces from ten to fifteen inches of rain in the west to as much as sixty inches of rain in the Lesser Kabylia

Opposite top: The oued *(streams) provide irrigation water for this vineyard. Opposite bottom: The Sahara Atlas Mountains are the source of many oued.*

16

Mountains in the east. Little rain falls in the summer, but the Mediterranean keeps the coastland very humid. Away from the sea, the rest of the Tell has less rainfall. Most of the rain falls in the mountains.

The Saharan Atlas Mountains, too, receive more rainfall than do the high plateaus, reaching an annual high of twenty-four inches compared to a low of eight or less in the plateaus.

Parts of the Sahara may go for years without a drop of rain, and then a sudden storm can bring an inch of moisture in a single downpour. The average high temperature in the Sahara during the summer is a miserably hot 120 degrees Fahrenheit, and days in the winter are only slightly cooler. But at night the desert temperature often drops to a dry, humidity-free 70 degrees, which seems very cold after the high daytime temperatures.

The high plateaus and the Tell both average about 80 degrees in the summer and from 40 to 50 degrees in the winter. Below-freezing temperatures are not uncommon during the high-plateau winters, and snow often falls in the Tell, especially in the higher altitudes. Along the coast, the sea usually keeps the temperature above freezing in the winter. Temperatures over 100 degrees and continued, very high humidity are normal during the summer.

Often much of Algeria, especially the high plateaus, is whipped by *sirocco* winds. This hot and dry wind blows northward from the desert and carries with it choking sand and dust. The sirocco winds occur from twenty to forty days a year, usually in the summer. Often these powerful winds cross the Mediterranean Sea and reach southern Italy and France. The sirocco is well known for the depression, unease, and general bad feeling that occurs among the people while it is blowing.

Three Children of Algeria

MOHAMMED OF ALGIERS

Mohammed was born on the very same day that Algeria achieved its independence from France—but in a different year. So every July 5, he and his family have a double celebration—Mohammed's birthday and Algeria's independence day.

Mohammed's father was an active fighter in the National Liberation Front (FLN) during the harsh and bloody eight-year-long war for independence. After the war, the FLN became Algeria's only political party. Mohammed's father has held important posts in various governmental departments. At present he works in the Ministry of Foreign Affairs.

Because Mohammed's father is well educated and has a good-paying political job, the family is able to live in a new apartment building near the top of the hill on which the capital city, Algiers, is built. Looking down from their windows, they can see the older parts of the city, with narrow, twisting streets and closely packed buildings. Farther below is the dark blue

of the Mediterranean Sea, with its chaotic mixture of port facilities—piers and docks of all sizes that are visited by a churning mass of large and small boats.

Mohammed's family is typical of the modern Algerians who live in the cities and larger towns of the country. Their lives and customs are a mixture of today's Western civilization and the ancient customs of their Islamic religion and their cultural heritage.

For example, Mohammed's clothes look like those belonging to any boy in Europe and the Americas—shirts, sweaters, trousers, and jackets. His father wears a business suit, but he also sometimes dons a *fez*—a cone-shaped cap often worn by Muslim men in Mediterranean countries. His mother wears Western-style dresses and shoes, but when she goes into public places, she usually wears the traditional *haik* over her head. Some haiks are long pieces of cloth that hang down to cover the entire body, but hers is short—just long enough to wrap around her face to serve as a veil.

The fez and the haik are typical pieces of Muslim wearing apparel. Mohammed and his family are strong believers in Islam, the Muslim religion. They believe "There is no God but Allah, and Muhammad is his Prophet." Muhammad lived in the city of Mecca (in present-day Saudi Arabia) many centuries ago. He founded Islam. Many of the events of their daily life are dictated by their beliefs. Five times

a day—at sunrise, noon, midafternoon, sunset, and nightfall—Mohammed kneels down on a prayer rug, faces east toward Mecca, and prays to Allah.

In the past, faithful Muslims were called to prayer five times a day by the cries of *muezzins.* Today the calls are usually recorded and broadcast by loudspeakers from *mosques,* the Muslim places of worship. Each Friday Mohammed and his father pray at the local mosque. There men and women worship in separate sections.

Islam prohibits drinking alcoholic beverages, eating pork, gambling, and smoking. Like his father, Mohammed has made a vow never to break these bans.

Fasting is also an important part of Islam. During Ramadan, the ninth month of the Muslim calendar (which is based on the lunar year), faithful Muslims fast all day long. The traditional way of telling when the day is over and night has fallen is to hold a black thread and a white thread side by side. When it is so dark that one cannot tell the colors of the two threads, the day has ended. The people can then eat until the next morning. The month of Ramadan ends with a three-day holiday, during which Muslims celebrate with feasts and prayers.

Each Muslim, if possible, should make a pilgrimage to Mecca once in his lifetime. Mohammed's father made a pilgrimage in 1963, just after Algeria became independent and just before he was married to Mohammed's mother. Often he has told his

Algiers, where Mohammed and his family live, is the largest city in Algeria.

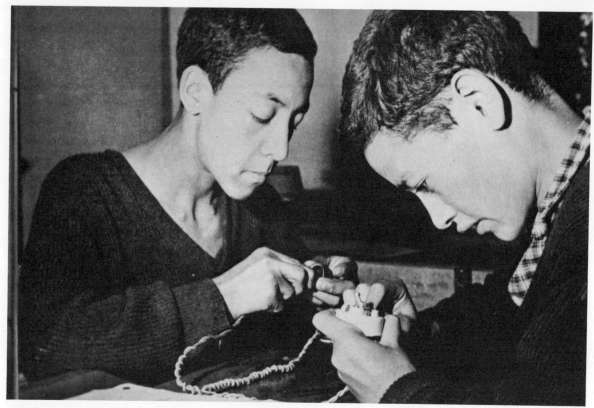

These boys, in a university-preparatory school, are studying the theory of electricity.

son of the special rites and prayers held for pilgrims in the holy city. He has promised that when Mohammed finishes his schooling, he will take him and his mother to Mecca for this most sacred of events in the life of a Muslim.

Almost every Algerian is a Muslim, but not all of them follow the rules of Islam as faithfully as do Mohammed and his family. At the university-preparatory school that Mohammed has entered recently, he has met many boys who smoke, who often break fasts during the month of Ramadan, and who seldom kneel down when they

pray. Strict adherence to the laws of Islam is fading in modern-day Algeria, but many families such as Mohammed's continue to follow the basic doctrines and rituals.

FATIMA OF MEDEA

About two hundred miles south of Algiers in a section of the country known as the high plateaus, sits a tiny village in the *wilaya* (district) of Medea, also called Titteri. The land around the village is flat and monotonous, broken only by a few curving hills in the distance. The sun beats down fiercely, and the only natural vegetation is sparse tufts of wild grass. The people of the village raise sheep and goats and tend small gardens of vegetables on the outskirts of the village.

The two dozen or so houses that make up the village are built around a well, from which Fatima draws water early in the morning. The houses are built close to one another, with courtyards enclosed by walls. The only other building in the town is a small mosque. The market is simply an open spot at one end of the village's single, narrow street.

The water that Fatima draws from the well has been tested by the government and found not to be contaminated. But the village has no sewer system, and garbage is dumped at a spot just outside the limits of the village. There are rats around the dump, and at night they can be heard scuttling through the village.

Although Fatima and all the other residents of her village are Muslims, they have some beliefs that would be looked on as primitive by the more sophisticated people of the urban sections of Algeria. Fatima is very afraid of meeting someone with the "evil eye." Such a person, she believes, could bring bad luck or perhaps even cause death simply by looking a person directly in the eye. To counteract the "evil eye," Fatima wears several charms and amulets that her mother gave her. When strangers come to the village (which seldom happens), Fatima makes certain never to look them directly in the eye.

ALGERIA AND TUNIS

The major building in small villages like Medea is the mosque.

The charms Fatima wears also keep away the spirits of the supernatural world that she believes can make a person ill. It is believed that these spirits are especially active at night. When Fatima has to venture outside after dark, she is certain to wear her charms and to speak special magical phrases to keep the spirits away.

All Algerian children are supposed to go to school for eight years. But no school has yet been built in or near Fatima's village, so it is likely that Fatima will never have this opportunity.

The people of Fatima's village wear the traditional Arab clothing. The modern dress common in Algiers has not been accepted yet in most rural areas of Algeria.

The men of Fatima's village wear several layers of garments—a short shirt, covered by another shirt that reaches the knees, and then a capelike shirt of cotton (in summer) or wool (in winter) that reaches the ankles. Over these the men wear an outer garment called a *burnous,* which is a loose cape worn over the shoulders. It can be pulled over the head and face as protection against sun, wind, or rain.

Fatima, her sisters, and her mother wear long, full-length haiks over several loose dresses. Their white haiks cover their heads; when the women are in public, they fling a fold of the haik over one shoulder so that it covers the lower half of their face. This follows the tradition of most Muslim countries, where women in public are covered completely except for their eyes.

In some Arab communities, women are seldom seen in public. But in Fatima's small village, women must help herd the sheep and goats and sometimes even work the fields of vegetables the villagers try to grow in the dry soil of their region.

Traditionally, women are considered the inferior sex in Algeria and in all other Arab nations. Since boys and girls do not work or play together, most marriages are arranged by parents or professional marriage matchmakers. It is quite likely that Fatima will be married when she is in her early teens. Then she will live in the house or village of her husband and will honor

These women are wearing full-length haiks, *a common item of clothing in Algeria.*

him as being stronger and more disciplined than she and entitled to being cared for and catered to. When she bears her husband's first child, Fatima will for the first time in her life receive a measure of respect—particularly if that child is a son.

Sooner or later, women in Algeria will not be forced to lead such a closed, cautious life as Fatima does. Already in Algiers and other cities, women are going to school, getting jobs, and entering the mainstream of life. But it will be many decades before such new patterns are accepted by the people of rural Algeria.

AHMED OF THE SAHARA

Deep in the southeastern section of Algeria, in the region of the Ahaggar Mountains, lives a group of wandering people called Tuaregs. At one time, they controlled almost all of the Sahara in Algeria. But when the French took over the country in the 1800s, they were pushed back into this corner of the desert. Only a few thousand Tuaregs remain in Algeria today; many more of them live in the two neighboring nations to the south—Niger and Mali. Isolated groups of Tuaregs live in many other central African countries.

The Tuaregs of Algeria are nomads who raise camels and sheep. They travel in small groups or clans on an eternal search for grass and water to feed their animals. Each clan consists of several nuclear family units (parents and children), and each family has its own sheepskin tent stretched over poles.

The Tuareg clan to which Ahmed be-

A young Algerian shepherd tends his flock of sheep.

longs has been moving slowly toward the oasis town of Tamanrasset. There they will sell some of their animals and buy foodstuffs and other provisions. Ahmed looks forward to his visit to Tamanrasset. There his clan will pitch their tents for an extended period of time just outside the town. Some of the family units will build small, temporary wooden huts covered with grass to replace their tents. Sooner or later, however, they will move on again, wandering the desert as their ancestors did many centuries ago.

Like most of the Arabs of Algeria, the Tuaregs are Berbers, descendants of the people who lived in what is now Algeria many thousands of years ago. They, too, are Muslims, but unlike 80 percent of the people of Algeria, they are not actively part of Arab culture. They speak a different language, do not intermarry with the Arabs, and take pride in the individuality of their culture and life.

Ahmed will probably never learn to read or write, for the Algerian government has built few schools in the desert. When schools are built, they have dormitories for the Tuareg children to live in. And in Tuareg culture, only women learn the Tuareg dialect's alphabet of twenty-four characters. No one in Ahmed's clan can speak either Arabic or French, Algeria's two most-used languages, and none of the men can read or write.

Tuareg women are different from most

Some of the more westernized Tuareg people work in oil refineries like this one.

MINISTRY OF INFORMATION

Muslim women in several other ways. They are not required to veil their faces, although sometimes they fold a portion of their outer garments across their faces to protect themselves from harsh weather. It is the Tuareg men who are veiled—by a blue turbanlike hood that covers all of the face except the eyes. Ahmed eats and sleeps while wearing his veil, and he would feel naked both in public and in the privacy of his family tent without it.

Ahmed's life as a Tuareg is different in many other ways from that of other Algerians. He will not marry at an early age— he may be thirty years old or more before he takes a wife—and he will choose his wife himself, without the help of his parents or a matchmaker. The Tuaregs have a *matriarchal* society, which means that Ahmed will inherit property from his mother's side of the family, not from his father's.

Ahmed spends most of each day helping his father and the other men of the clan with the sheep and camels. That is about all the work Tuareg men do; they are brought up to believe that it is improper for men to do manual labor. Women and servants do all of the work in the camp.

Although he is a citizen of the republic of Algeria, Ahmed feels much closer to other Tuaregs—even those in Mali and Niger—than he does to other Algerians. The modern world, however, is intruding even into the Sahara. Although Ahmed's life may follow the pattern of his father's life, it is likely that Ahmed's children will have more contact with other Algerians.

Already some Tuaregs have bought or rented farmland outside of oasis towns. Quite a few Tuareg men have taken jobs in the oil and natural gas fields of eastern Algeria. The Trans-Saharan Road, which will cut across the desert through the town of Tamanrasset, will bring new jobs and new contacts with modern life to the Tuaregs. By the time Ahmed is married and is a father, more Tuareg children may attend school, learn to speak and read Arabic, and settle down permanently in some towns or villages.

It will not be many decades before the nomadic life that Ahmed knows will disappear, as will the cloistered life of Muslim women that Fatima knows. The strict Muslim beliefs of Mohammed and his family also will be modified as Algeria participates more and more in world affairs. The children of Algeria may try to cling to their customs, cultures, and religion as they grow older, but the influence of technology and modern civilization is unstoppable. As Algeria becomes an industrialized society, its people will meet and accept the challenges of that society. Today's Algerian children are probably the last of their kind.

Algeria Yesterday

CARTHAGE AND ROME

Algeria's earliest recorded history cannot be separated from that of its neighbors, Morocco and Tunisia. For about two thousand years, various kingdoms, empires, and city-states of the Mediterranean area ruled the people of northwestern Africa.

The earliest-known people of Algeria were wandering tribes who drove cattle and sheep from place to place looking for water and vegetation. Later they came to be known as Berbers. Europeans gave the name "Barbary," or Barbary Coast, to all of Africa north of the Sahara, because of the Berbers.

The first foreign intruders into Algeria were probably the Phoenicians, from the far eastern Mediterranean. They set up ports and trading posts all along the sea over twelve centuries ago. One of the most important Phoenician trading posts was Carthage, built in about 800 B.C. at what is now the city of Tunis. For six hundred years, the city-state of Carthage ruled the ports of the North African coast. With the cooperation of the Berber leaders, Carthage founded trading posts on what is now the Algerian coast and introduced agricultural methods to the Berbers, making some of their constant nomadic traveling unnecessary.

The Carthaginians fought the Roman Empire, headquartered directly across the Mediterranean Sea, for control of the trade and riches of the lands around the Mediterranean. A Berber chief named Massinissa aided the Romans in their war

The arch of Caracalla is a reminder of Algeria's past.

against Carthage. For assisting Rome, Massinissa won the independent kingdom of Numidia, which consisted of most of Algeria north of the Sahara.

After Carthage's destruction (it was later rebuilt) by the Romans in 146 B.C., Rome tried to increase its influence in Numidia. The Berbers revolted with Massinissa's grandson, Jugurtha, as their leader. However, they were defeated by the Romans. Eventually all of North Africa, including Numidia, was annexed to the Roman Empire.

In 313 A.D. the Roman emperor Constantine I made Christianity the official religion of his empire. He named a North African Berber Christian as bishop of Hippo (present-day Annaba). That man became a great influence in the Roman Catholic Church; he is known today as St. Augustine.

VANDALS AND BYZANTINES

By the fourth century A.D., Rome's power was weakening. A tribe known as the Vandals came sweeping down from what is now Germany. Led by their king, Genseric, they fought their way through Gaul (now France) and Spain, and captured Rome. In 430 A.D. two hundred thousand of Genseric's Vandals sailed a mighty fleet from Spain to what is now Morocco. Nine years later they had forced their way eastward and had captured Carthage. Soon the Vandals controlled all of North Africa and much of the Mediterranean Sea.

The Vandal occupation lasted for almost exactly one hundred years. During that time, the Byzantine Empire was gaining power in the eastern Mediterranean. Sometimes called the Eastern Roman Empire, and headquartered in the city of Byzantium (now Istanbul in Turkey), it was a successor to the defeated Roman empire that had been centered in what is now Italy. Under Emperor Justinian I, the Byzantine general Belisarius drove out the Vandals from North Africa in 534 A.D.

The Byzantine occupation also lasted for about a century. The Berber peoples never fully accepted the cultures of either the Vandals or the Byzantines, who were both essentially European. It was not until Arab armies began to arrive in North Africa—in the mid-seventh century—that the Berbers were strongly influenced by a foreign culture.

ARABS AND MUSLIMS

In 632 A.D. the Prophet Muhammad died, having founded a new religion called Islam. His followers, known as Muslims, began to spread the religion. They reached North Africa around 670 A.D. Though the Berbers resisted these new invaders, by the beginning of the eighth century, they were finally conquered.

Little by little, the Berbers began to accept the Arab domination. When three factions of Muslims fought for control in the Arab world, most of the Berbers of what is now Algeria joined the Kharidjite sect in

The intricate patterns and bright colors of the tapestry (left), the designs on the pottery (below left), and the intricate metal work of the jewelry (below) all reveal, to the trained eye, pieces of Algeria's long and varied cultural history.

These Berbers, unlike their ancestors of past centuries, live in harmony with the Arabs of Algeria.

protest against the Arab rule. By the year 800, the Kharidjite Berbers had thrown off the political domination of the invading Arabs—but had accepted firmly their Muslim religion.

For the next several centuries, various Muslim sects or dynasties fought for control over present-day Algeria. The Kharidjites were defeated in 911 by a new branch of the Islam religion called Shia and ruled by the Fatimids, who took their name from Fatima, the Prophet Muhammad's daughter. Some Berbers still resisted the Fatimids, who ruled from Cairo (Egypt). The Fatimids responded by sending thousands and thousands of members of their sect to settle in present-day Algeria. This immense immigration continued for several

hundred years. During this time, the Berbers gradually began to speak the Arab language and intermarry with the Arabs. Slowly, the character of the people of today's Algeria began to form.

Different Muslim sects, however, still battled for control of North Africa—first the Almoravids, then the Almohads gaining control of what is now Algeria.

SPAIN AND PIRATES

Spain had been conquered in the eighth century by the Arabs, whom the Spanish called Moors. About seven hundred years later, in the year 1492, several important historical events occurred in Spain. The last Muslim Arabs were driven from Spain, and Christianity once again became the nation's religion. King Ferdinand V and Queen Isabella I united most of the country. Muslims and Jews who were expelled from Spain crossed the Mediterranean to take refuge in the coastal North African cities, including those in Algeria. And Christopher Columbus sailed westward and found a new world.

By the early sixteenth century, Spain controlled many of the port cities of North Africa. Although it never captured the port of Algiers, it successfully dominated the city by occupying an offshore island. In desperation, the Arab ruler of Algiers called for assistance from infamous Turkish pirates who had been making daring attacks on ports all over the Mediterranean area.

Two pirate brothers named Barbarossa (Redbeard) came to the aid of Algiers. The first, Arudj, took over as commander of the city. When he was killed, his brother Khair al Din replaced him and made Algiers a regency of the powerful Ottoman Empire based in the Turkish city of Constantinople. The Ottoman Empire was the successor to the Eastern Roman (Byzantine) Empire and Constantinople was the new name for the old city of Byzantium, now Istanbul. Finally the Spanish were forced from Penon Island in 1518, although they continued to control the Algerian city of Oran for 250 more years.

In 1518 Khair al Din named himself Algeria's ruler, as representative of the Turkish sultan. For the next three hundred years, Algeria was a province of the Ottoman Empire, governed by *deys,* or chiefs. Algeria was divided into smaller regions ruled by *beys,* or governors, who collected taxes.

The name "Algiers" is derived from the Arabic words *el jazair* ("the islands") which referred to islands in the harbor of the port city. Soon the Turks referred to the entire regency as Algeria, and its people as Algerians.

Algiers became the capital of the ships that scoured the coast of North Africa. They attacked many European sailing vessels, stealing their cargoes and taking slaves. The captains and crews of these pirate ships (as they were called by the Europeans) demanded tributes from Europe-

The port of Algiers, today the country's main seaport, was once the home of the Barbary pirates.

an nations in return for allowing their ships to sail the Mediterranean without being attacked.

During the Turkish rule, the Berbers of Algeria continued to live their lives as they had previously. Attempts at insurrections were cruelly put down by the Turks. It was to take the actions of two other nations to "free" the Berbers from the Turks—but those actions only put them under the rule of yet another conqueror.

AMERICA AND FRANCE

In the early 1800s, the United States government reacted against the piracy along what had become known as the Barbary Coast. When William Bainbridge, the captain of an American ship, was insulted by the dey of Algiers, the U.S. unofficially declared war against the Barbary Turks.

The famous American naval captain Stephen Decatur took part in sea battles around Algiers. In 1815 he was able to force the Algerian dey to sign a treaty that ended the payment of U.S. tribute to the pirates.

But the Barbary Coast pirates continued their attacks on the European ships. France, whose influence had been growing in Algeria, blockaded the port of Algiers for three years, from 1827 to 1830. On July 5, 1830, it captured the city and expelled the dey. Within a few years, France had control over all the major North African ports. The days of the pirates were over. The Algerian coast was declared to

be a colony of France in 1834.

But occupation of the interior was another matter. Organized resistance to the French sprang up, led by various beys of the interior provinces. Soon the resistance turned into a full-scale *jihad,* or holy war, pitting the Muslim Algerians against the Christian French, whom the Muslims regarded as infidels.

The leader of the jihad against the French was one of the great heroes of Algerian history, Abdel Kader. He was only twenty-four years old in 1832 when he began what would become fifteen years of continued struggle against the French. An educated man, he was regarded as an *amir,* or prince, by the Algerian tribesmen.

It was a terrible war—on both sides. Abdel Kader wrote of the French: "We shall tire them, we shall harrass them, we shall destroy them bit by bit; the climate will do the rest." The French Minister of War's words were just as final: "We have to resign ourselves to . . . exterminating the native population. Plunder, burn, ruin the agriculture is perhaps the only means to solidly establish our domination."

In many ways, the war of resistance was like the final battle for Algerian independence would be more than a century later—except for the outcome. By 1847 the Algerians were outnumbered by more than one hundred thousand French soldiers. Abdel Kader surrendered in December of that year.

At first he was imprisoned in France, then exiled to Turkey, and later to Syria. There in 1860 he was responsible for saving twelve thousand Christians, including French officials, from massacre by the Turks. In return, the French honored their former enemy with the Legion of Honor award.

Abdel Kader never returned to public life. He died in Syria in 1883, a scholar and a man deeply devoted to helping the poor. In 1966, on the fourth anniversary of Algerian independence, his body was returned to Algeria with great ceremony and was enshrined in a mosque in Constantine. The mosque has become a national shrine to the people of Algeria.

COLONIALISM

As a French colony, Algeria's cities gradually became Europeanized, especially the coastal cities. Thousands of Europeans emigrated to Algeria—109,000 by 1847 and more than three times that number by 1881—and half of them were French. The immigrants took over governmental, business, and cultural control of the colony, driving the Algerians themselves back to the status of fourth-class citizens. After 1889 children born to Europeans automatically were declared French citizens. Berber lands were confiscated and much of them given to the European colonists. Native-born Algerians could not become French citizens unless they renounced their Muslim religion, and few of them did. Muslims who broke the law were punished more severely than were Europeans.

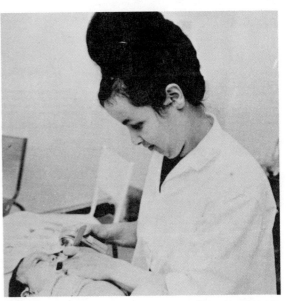

MINISTRY OF INFORMATION

The French were the first to bring Western medicine to Algeria.

Periodically, isolated Berber uprisings were put down harshly by the French army. The most serious revolt, led in 1871 by Mohammed El Hadj Mokrani, started from the mountains of the Kabylia. When it, too, was crushed, there were few large-scale rebellions for the next seventy-five years. However, it was not until about 1914 that the French completely occupied all of the Saharan region of Algeria.

Around the turn of the century, the French granted the native Algerians a minimum of freedom. Two Algerians were allowed to be named to an advisory committee to the French governor. A few Algerian children were admitted to French schools. Some Algerian civil servants were hired, but in general these were looked upon as traitors by their own people.

35

Unlike in colonial times, when few Algerian children were allowed to attend school, today all Algerian children have the right to an education.

THE SEEDS OF NATIONALISM

During World War I, many Algerians served in the French army or worked as laborers in France. There they became aware of the kind of freedom noncolonial life could offer. When they returned to Algeria after the war, they brought with them the seeds of Algerian nationalism.

In the nineteenth century, the battles against the French had been in the nature of a religious war—Muslims versus Christians. But the new attitude of Algerian nationalism was not wholly religious. It was a refusal to accept either French citizenship or domination by the French. It was a demand for equality and for a status as citizenship in Algeria alone. Yet it was understood that with this citizenship, the Muslim faith would be the supreme faith in Algeria.

In 1926 the Star of North Africa movement was founded by Messali Hadj as an anticolonialist group. The French banned the Star party and jailed Messali—he was to spend many years in prison for his anti-French leadership. But the Star soon gained widespread acceptance, especially among those who worked or had worked in France. By 1933 the Star was demanding independence, an all-Algerian government and army, and the right to vote.

The French were afraid to give in to any of Messali's demands, since all the European colonists, or *colons,* in Algeria in the mid-1930s numbered less than one million, compared to about eight million Algerian Muslims. When the Star of North Africa was banned again, Messali Hadj founded the Algerian People's Party (PPA) with the same anticolonial principles. It, too, was declared illegal, and Messali Hadj was arrested and jailed again.

WORLD WAR II

Early in World War II, northern France was occupied by German Nazi soldiers. Southern France and most of the overseas colonies (including Algeria) came under control of the so-called Vichy French government, which cooperated with the Germans.

Generally, the European colons in Algeria backed the Vichy government. But most of the Algerians themselves opposed it, especially when Jewish Algerians were deprived of their French citizenship and discriminated against in much the same manner as the Muslims had been for years.

Soon after British and American forces liberated Algeria late in 1942, the French called on the Muslims to help drive German forces from the rest of North Africa. A new nationalist spokesman, Ferhat Abbas, and fifty-six other anticolonialist leaders issued a manifesto demanding in return more freedom and equality for the Algerian Muslims. Under the leadership of exiled General Charles DeGaulle, the

French offered minor reforms, including French citizenship, to a group of about sixty thousand elite Algerians.

DeGaulle's offers fell far short of the nationalists' demands. Abbas and other Algerian leaders, with the backing of the still-imprisoned Messali Hadj, formed a new group, the Friends of the Manifesto and Liberty (AML). By the end of World War II, it claimed to have half a million supporters.

PRELUDE TO WAR

On May 8, 1945 (the day World War II ended in Europe), an event occurred that brought on the final break between the European colons and the native Muslim Algerians. Thousands of people in the town of Setif marched in celebration of the war's end. Among them were AML members who carried signs with nationalist slogans. French police tried to take away the signs. A scuffle broke out, then a full-scale riot. The news of the Setif riot spread to other cities, where smaller outbreaks of protest occurred. Looking back, there seems little doubt that the police overreacted, especially in post-riot repressions against the Algerians.

The final toll of the riots is uncertain, but about eighty-eight to one hundred Europeans were dead, and anywhere from fifteen hundred (the French figure) to forty-five thousand (the highest-recorded Algerian estimate) Algerians were killed. Many Algerians had been killed during

The struggle for independence involved all Algerians, including nomadic Bedouins like this man.

the period of repression, when the French navy and air force carried out bombardments and when truckloads of Algerians were driven away, executed, and buried in common graves. Thousands of other Algerians were arrested and imprisoned.

During the next few years, the French government in Paris attempted to quiet the political and nationalist fervor in Algeria. Whenever it gave in to even minor Algerian demands, it faced great resentment from the colons. In 1947 General DeGaulle, until then a great favorite with the Muslims, demanded that France remain in control of Algeria. With that demand, he lost the support of the Algerians but gained respect from French and other European colons.

For the next seven years, various Algerian organizations began planning rebellion, some openly and some secretly. Messali Hadj, released from prison in France after five years, formed a new party, the Movement for the Triumph of Democratic Liberties (MTLD). A group called the Secret Organization (OS) was formed within the party to carry on terrorist activities against the colons. Eventually it was headed by Ahmed Ben Bella.

In 1952 Messali Hadj was arrested again and deported to France. Never again was he to return to an important position in Algerian nationalism. Other leaders and other organizations took his place, and Messali Hadj died in exile in France in 1974.

By 1954 most of the nationalist groups had joined together to form the National Liberation Front (FLN), a political faction, and the National Liberation Army (ALN), a military operation. Together the FLN and ALN planned full-scale guerrilla warfare against the French.

THE REVOLUTION

The Algerian war for independence started shortly after midnight on the morning of November 1, 1954. ALN guerrillas attacked seventy French military posts, mainly in the area of the Aures Mountains. The long period of armed revolt had begun.

Within two years, the forces of the ALN had grown from three thousand to fifty thousand men. Algerians everywhere rallied to the cause of independence, and

Time has erased most of the evidence of the fierce fighting that took place in Algiers during the struggle for independence.

the number of incidents of military attack, bombing, sabotage, and assassination increased.

The French colons reacted to the wave of terror by using force against the rebellious Algerians. By late 1956 the FLN directed an average of seven hundred acts of terror in Algiers each month. By this time, the French army in Algeria had been increased to four hundred thousand men. Several of the top FLN leaders, including Ben Bella, were captured and imprisoned. But the war continued.

During the so-called Battle of Algiers, from December 1956 to September 1957, the French army and police used extremely brutal measures, including torture, to destroy all traces of the FLN in the city. The army claimed to be using methods no worse than those practiced by the FLN. But throughout the world, in the United Nations, and even in France itself, a great protest against French brutality began to arise, as well as a great demand for Algerian freedom.

Some ALN forces had been training and taking refuge in neighboring Morocco and Tunisia. Although the French built electrified wire fences along the borders, this did little to stop people from getting through. Many Algerians were put in prisons or concentration camps from 1957 to 1960—perhaps as many as two million.

The Algerian colons and French army were afraid that France would grant independence to its colony, thus destroying the minority power they long had held. They threatened to break away completely from the mother country. Feelings on both sides of the issue were so strong that they brought down the French government in Paris, and late in 1958 Charles DeGaulle was elected president of France. This satisfied the colons and the army, as DeGaulle had insisted that Algeria must remain a colony of France.

DeGaulle offered the Muslim Algerians many political, economic, and social reforms and called for a cease-fire. But the FLN turned down his offers and once again increased its campaign of terrorism. And once again the French army increased its tactics of repression.

Late in 1959 DeGaulle changed his policy completely. He offered the Algerians the promise of independence, if they voted for it, once peace had been restored. This led many colons and soldiers to revolt in Algiers in January of 1960. These extremists, dead set against independence, began a terrorist campaign similar to that of the FLN. Bombs were set off in public places in both Algeria and France. The campaign was led by a retired French general, Raoul Salan, who called his organization of colon rebels the Secret Army Organization (OAS). France was on the verge of civil war.

Throughout 1960 and 1961, the three-sided warfare continued. The French army, loyal to DeGaulle, tried to cope with the terrorism of both the FLN and OAS. Meanwhile, during 1961, FLN leaders were meeting in Evian, France, with French government officials to try to bring about peace.

INDEPENDENCE

Finally, on March 18, 1962, a cease-fire agreement was signed at Evian. A vote for or against independence was promised the Algerians, and the FLN was recognized as the political spokesparty of the colony.

Despite a final, desperate OAS terrorist campaign, the referendum was held on July 1. More than 99 percent of the Algerians voted for independence. Algeria was declared independent on July 3, but the leaders of the revolution named July 5, 1962, as Independence Day. It was the 132nd anniversary of the French capture of Algiers.

The war had left at least one-tenth of Algeria's total population of ten million dead or missing. Up to three million Muslims had been imprisoned or had taken refuge in neighboring countries or the interior of Algeria. And by the end of 1962, OAS members and most of the colons had fled to France. Only about 250,000 Europeans remained in Algeria.

Algeria Today

BEGINNING

In the early 1960s, Algeria faced two major problems—economy and politics. These were problems common to almost all of the newly independent nations of Africa in that decade. When Algeria had been a colony, the colons had controlled its business, industry, trade, and agriculture. When most of the colons fled after independence, the new nation's economy nearly came to a stop.

Two of the FLN leaders, Ahmed Ben Bella and Benyoussef Ben Khedda, vied for control of the new government. Immediately after independence, Ben Khedda set himself up as premier in Algiers. A week later, Ben Bella, the deputy premier, and Houari Boumediene, former commander of the ALN, set up a separate government in Tlemcen.

On September 9, 1962, Boumediene led an army of seven thousand loyal troops into Algiers. An election for members of a National Assembly took place on September 20. Not surprisingly, Ben Bella and his supporters won.

The Assembly, of course, elected Ben Bella premier. His cabinet included Boumediene as defense minister. Opposing political factions, including the Communist Party, were banned. By the end of 1962, Ben Bella's government had been recognized by the rest of the world and had gained membership in the Arab League and the United Nations. In April of 1963, Algeria helped found the Organization of African Unity (OAU).

Modern-day Algiers is a busy, thriving city with many new buildings.

BEGINNING AGAIN

Under a constitution adopted by the National Assembly in September 1963, Ben Bella was elected president of the Democratic and Popular Republic of Algeria for a five-year term. He also served as leader of the armed forces. The constitution stipulated that Algeria have one official language—Arabic, one official religion—Islam, and one official political party—the FLN.

Ben Bella set out to make Algeria important in world affairs. He got loans and technical assistance from the USSR and the World Bank. He set up a unity committee with neighboring Morocco and Tunisia. He backed revolutions in other African colonies that had not yet gained independence. And he tried to export his brand of socialism, called *autogestion,* in which workers and farmers in any particular business control the management.

But at home in Algeria, many began to feel that Ben Bella was spending too much time on foreign affairs. They also began to look upon him as a dictator. So Ben Bella broke with other former FLN leaders and the labor unions. He even tried to weaken the power of the army by setting up a citizens' militia, thereby losing the friendship of his long-time associate, Houari Boumediene.

Late in June of 1965, a conference of African and Asian nations was to meet in Algiers. This event would have increased Ben Bella's prestige immensely, but it never took place. On June 19, in a quick bloodless coup, Ben Bella was arrested and imprisoned. A Council of Revolution replaced the National Assembly and shortly afterward named Houari Boumediene as president. The leader's former right-hand man had taken power.

A NEW LEADER

Little was known in 1965—or is known now—about the early life of Houari Boumediene. His real name was Muhammad Boukharouba, but he had changed it during the war for independence. He was thought to have been born in either 1925 or 1927, making him thirty-eight or forty years old when he assumed power. He was educated mainly at Constantine and then at Al-Azhar University in Cairo.

While in Egypt in the mid-1950s, Boumediene joined a group of Algerian nationalists. He began to study military tactics, first in Egypt and then in Morocco, and by 1957 was commander of the revolutionary guerrillas in western Algeria. By the time of independence, he commanded the ALN from headquarters in Tunisia.

When he became president, Boumediene suspended Algeria's three-year-old constitution and ruled with the approval of the Council of Revolution. Besides being president, he also became premier and minister of defense, making Houari Boumediene Algeria's governmental, political, and military leader.

The new president continued many of Ben Bella's policies but soon showed a

Houari Boumediene became president of Algeria in 1965.

greater knowledge of, and interest in, affairs within Algeria. Although Algeria continued to receive aid from the Soviet Union, Boumediene refused to align Algeria exclusively with either the Communist or non-Communist nations. He also entered a new arrangement of cooperation with France, which Ben Bella had refused to do.

At home Boumediene continued the socialist policy of autogestion but assured the people that private enterprise would not be abolished. His cabinet of ministers represented all phases of Algerian life and politics, not just the FLN. His prime objective was to improve Algeria economically.

Boumediene, unlike Ben Bella, wanted to help the people of Algeria, not impress the rest of the world. In general, Algerians approved of him and his policies.

NEW LAWS

Although the constitution remained suspended, Boumediene set out to bring the people of Algeria into the decision-making processes of government. The French had divided Algeria into fifteen *departments,* governing districts similar to states in the United States. In 1967 the nation was divided further into 676 *communes* (similar to U.S. counties). Each commune elected a

People's Assembly to govern and to make decisions in social, cultural, and economic fields. In communal assembly elections in 1967 and 1971, the FLN remained the only political party on the ballot, but two candidates from the party ran for each seat.

To decentralize federal governmental power, the Wilaya Code was decreed in 1969. It set up fifteen *wilayas,* or administrative districts, which were declared to be "the meeting-places for the harmonization of local interests and national requirements." (The wilayas are similar to the states of the United States, the communes similar to counties.) The wilayas had the same boundaries as the departments set up by the French had had.

Before and after independence, Algeria's major industries were controlled by foreign firms, mainly French. Boumediene announced in 1968 that Algeria would nationalize (take over and operate) all foreign-owned companies, especially those involving mineral resources. By 1971 more than half of all the French oil companies had been nationalized, as well as all the French natural gas and pipeline properties. The foreign owners would be compensated.

In 1970 Boumediene announced a Four-Year Plan for the economic development of Algeria, to improve the nation's industry and agriculture. This would lower the unemployment rate and make Algeria less dependent on other nations for imported goods and services.

At first the Four-Year Plan concentrated on manufacturing and mining. But in 1971 the Agrarian Revolution began; it aimed at progress in Algeria's ability to grow its own food. Cooperative farms were set up for rural peasants—the land had been nationalized from farms run by absentee owners and large estates owned by individual European families.

At times early in Boumediene's presidency, some former FLN officials who disagreed with his policies made halfhearted attempts to replace him. But the Algerian army remained loyal to its commander-in-chief, and the attempted coups failed. In April of 1968, the car in which Boumediene was riding was hit by machine-gun fire. However, the president was only slightly injured.

NEW RECOGNITION

Before long, Boumediene was recognized as one of the most important leaders in the Arab world. He sought, unsuccessfully, to form a North African federation of four Arab nations—Libya, Mauritania, Tunisia, and Algeria. In November 1973, he hosted a conference of the fifteen Arab nations that joined together in backing the Arab side in the continuing Arab-Israeli crisis. Algeria joined with other oil-rich Arab nations late in 1973 in raising the

Both the mining (opposite top) and natural-gas (opposite bottom) industries were nationalized by Boumediene's government.

Abdel-Aziz Bouteflika began a one-year term as president of the United Nations General Assembly in September 1974.

price of oil and then embargoing (holding back) oil shipments to some European countries and the United States. This group called itself OPEC (Organization of Petroleum Exporting Countries).

Soon Boumediene came to be recognized not only as a spokesman for Arab nations but also for the nations of the so-called Third World. (The "Third World" comprised those underdeveloped nations that were not formally aligned with either the Communist or non-Communist world.)

Representatives of seventy-six Third World nations met outside Algiers at the new Palace of Nations in 1973. They had gathered for the fourth Summit Conference of Non-Aligned Countries. At the conference, Boumediene called for "true economic liberation" and "political independence" for the attending nations, which included states as diverse as India, Yugoslavia, Malta, Ethiopia, and Cambodia.

Early in 1974 Boumediene made his first trip to the United States, to address a special session of the United Nations General Assembly. Again he called for the rapid industrialization of the Third World nations and urged them to nationalize foreign-owned business firms.

Algeria's importance in world affairs was recognized when its foreign minister, Abdel-Aziz Bouteflika, was elected president of the UN General Assembly in September of 1974. Bouteflika had worked with Boumediene during the revolution and had served in the cabinet of ministers since independence. With his support, the other Third World nations in the UN formed an effective bloc that for the first time in UN history successfully opposed former powers such as the United States, the USSR, and Great Britain.

NEW PROGRESS

The mid-1970s saw a flurry of activities that increased Algeria's influence throughout the world and sought to create better

This textile factory (left) and heavy-equipment factory (right) are two of the new industries in Algeria that provide both jobs and economic growth for this nation.

living conditions for its people at home.

In foreign affairs, Algeria and other member countries of OPEC maintained their price for oil. President Boumediene warned the large industrial countries against using their power to lower prices.

Algeria restored its diplomatic relations with the United States in 1974. The relations had been broken at the time of the 1967 Arab-Israeli War.

In internal affairs, another four-year plan, this time called the Industrial Revolution, was set up in 1974. This plan aimed at making Algeria self-sufficient in the manufacture and sale of industrial products.

Another "revolution" was started in the mid-1970s. This one was termed the Socialist Revolution, and it aimed at bringing more people into politics and political decisions. The announcement was made as part of the twentieth anniversary of the beginning of Algeria's battle for independence from France.

The first of six billion seedling trees were planted to inaugurate the "Green Belt," a twenty-year project designed to prevent the Sahara from moving northward.

The first French president to visit Algeria since independence, Valery Giscard d'Estaing, met with President Boumediene in Algiers in 1975. Now dependent on its former colony for oil, France was seeking to improve diplomatic and trade relations.

By the mid-1970s, after little more than a decade of independence, Algeria and its president had become international symbols of the growing power of the Arab, the nonaligned, and the oil-producing nations. At home the agrarian, industrial, and socialist revolutions were beginning to bring a better standard of living to many Algerians.

The long centuries of occupation by and warfare with the Carthaginians, Romans, Vandals, Byzantines, Arabs, Turks, and French had faded away into history. Algeria seemed well on its way to introducing the positive changes that would bring forth progress.

GOVERNMENT

The constitution of 1963 called for three equal governmental bodies—legislative (the National Assembly), executive (the president and the Council of Ministers), and judicial (the courts). The president and representatives to the National Assembly arc elected by the people. The Council of Ministers (presidential cabinet) are appointed by the president.

After Boumediene's coup in 1965, the constitution was suspended until a new one could be adopted. The National Assembly was abolished and replaced by a Council of Revolution. No federal elections were held.

Before long, the power of the Council of Revolution was transferred unofficially to the Council of Ministers. This Council does not pass laws but issues decrees. The twenty cabinet ministries include defense, interior, health, tourism, foreign affairs, finance, agriculture, and justice.

As president, Houari Boumediene presides over both the Council of Revolution and the Council of Ministers. He also holds the post of Minister of Defense, which gives him control of the armed forces.

The Minister of Interior supervises the fifteen wilayas. Each wilaya is headed by a governor (appointed by the Minister of Interior) and a Wilaya Assembly (elected by the people).

The 676 communes are the basic level of local government. Communal assemblies, elected by the people, carry on the everyday governing of the communes.

Assembly elections are similar to those provided by the suspended constitution, with one major exception. Anyone older than eighteen years of age who is a registered voter can cast a ballot. However, only candidates of the FLN Party are on the ballot—two candidates for each assembly post.

Algeria's court system is still based primarily on the French code of law. Little by little, however, the principles of Islamic law are being incorporated into the system.

Justices of the peace sit as judges at the communal level. Above them in jurisdiction are Lower Courts and Wilaya Courts, one in each wilaya capital. The highest court of appeal is the Supreme Court, but it cannot rule on whether executive decrees are legal. The entire court system is under

This woman, wearing the traditional haik, *casts her ballot in a local election.*

the supervision of the Minister of Justice.

THE MILITARY

Besides defending the nation, Algeria's armed forces have an important role in the nation's economic and political life. At independence, the ALN (National Liberation Army) became the ANP (National People's Army). The ANP takes part in construction projects throughout Algeria and retains a strong political control. President Boumediene is the Minister of Defense and the commander-in-chief of the ANP.

In the mid-1970s, Algeria's total military strength was about sixty-five thousand, fifty-five thousand of whom were members of the army. The rest comprised the navy and the air force. The navy has bases along the Mediterranean; the air force has bases in northern Algeria.

Most of the ANP's equipment has come from the Soviet Union, but some equipment and training assistance has also come from France, the People's Republic of China, and Egypt.

51

EDUCATION

Part of the 1970 Four-Year Plan for Algeria's development called for at least one million people to become literate (able to read and write). Fewer than 20 percent of Algeria's total population, including colons, were said to be literate in 1954. Since independence, great strides and great amounts of money for education have barely been able to keep up with the rise in population. In the mid-1970s, the literacy rate was estimated to be at about 25 to 30 percent.

During the French occupation, most of the schools taught French subjects in the French language to French and other European children. Very few native-born Muslim children could speak French; thus very few were educated. In 1944 only 8 percent of the native Algerian children were able to attend "native" schools.

French policy was opposed to Algerian education. In the twenty years before independence, the French opened some schools for Muslims, with teaching in the Arabic language. But at independence, fewer than 30 percent of the primary and secondary school students were Muslims.

After independence schools were taught

These students learn to work with and repair complex communications equipment at the Telecommunications Training Center in Algiers.

in Arabic rather than French. But since there was a lack of Arabic-speaking teachers, this changeover took place gradually. By 1973 about 2.2 million students attended primary schools and 278,000 attended secondary schools—almost double the number in school in 1966.

Primary education is free and compulsory for children six to fourteen. But many children never attend school, especially those who live in rural areas.

The secondary-school system is based on the French system. There are two types of schools: four-year general schools and seven-year university-preparatory schools. Graduates of the preparatory schools must pass stiff examinations before being admitted to universities.

Despite a teacher-training program, there is still a shortage of teachers in Algeria. From 1966 to 1973, the total number of teachers in primary and secondary schools rose from about forty thousand to sixty thousand.

The oldest university in Algeria is the University of Algiers, founded by the French for French students in 1909. Two other universities were established after independence—one each in Oran and Constantine. Before independence fewer than one thousand university students were Algerian; in the 1970s, all university students were Algerians. Twenty-seven thousand students attended universities in Algeria in 1973.

Thirty-one technical and vocational schools specialize in courses such as agriculture, teacher training, journalism, engineering, public works, communications, and industrial training. People not able to attend school can study courses in general subjects by mail. Adult education by mail is also available.

Great strides have been made since independence in educating young and old alike. But it will be many more years before Algerians in all parts of the country will be able to go to school.

Natural Treasures

PLANT AND ANIMAL LIFE

Thousands of years ago, what is now Algeria was covered with fertile soil, running rivers, lush vegetation, and wild animals. At that time, the land resembled parts of today's central Africa.

Signs of that ancient land still remain. Rock paintings and engravings in the plateau areas of the southern Sahara show trees, rivers, and animals such as elephants, hippopotamuses, and crocodiles. Experts estimate that the rock pictures were made from three to nine thousand years ago. Later engravings show horses and camels—indications that domesticated animals were part of the life of the area from two to three thousand years ago.

But through the centuries, the desert took over much of northern Africa.

Changes in climate brought less and less rainfall. Eventually the animals and vegetation disappeared, and the Sahara began to grow. In Algeria the Sahara is still pushing slowly northward.

Today elephants, hippopotamuses, and crocodiles no longer live in Algeria. There are still some packs of wild carnivores, such as hyenas and jackals, monkeys, hawks, and desert snakes. But the animal life of ages past has been replaced with millions of head of grazing animals—cattle, sheep, goats, horses, camels, and mules.

In northern Algeria, where rainfall is heaviest, grow olive and citrus trees, Aleppo pines, cork and evergreen oaks, firs, and poplars. Most of the cedar trees that once grew there disappeared long ago, cut down for fuel and building material.

Oil is by far the most profitable of any of Algeria's natural resources.

Date palms grow in profusion wherever there is a desert oasis. They provide both food and shelter from the sun.

Farther south, away from the Mediterranean, trees grow only on the upper slopes of the mountains, where some pines, junipers, oaks, and cedars can be found. On the high plateaus, vegetation is limited to scrub pines, oaks, and wild grass used for grazing.

In the desert itself, there is practically no vegetation except near the oases, where palm trees are cultivated for their dates. When an occasional brief rainfall spatters in the dry, sandy soil, tiny desert plants that have remained dormant for years may suddenly spring to life for a short period of time, perhaps even sending forth rare, blossoming flowers.

To stop the northward drift of the desert, work has begun on a project as impressive as the building of the Egyptian pyramids. In January 1975, planting began on a "Green Belt" of trees. The belt will stretch across Algeria from Morocco to Tunisia, just south of the Saharan Atlas and Aures mountain chains. Eventually a barrier

The "Green Belt" project, which will require the growing and re-planting of billions of seedling trees, is a massive undertaking designed to stop the desert from moving farther north.

forest will separate the Tell and high plateaus of northern Algeria from the Sahara. Most of the trees to be planted will be Aleppo and eucalyptus pines, which are thought to be able to thrive in the sandy soil and hot climate.

The statistics of the "Green Belt" project are almost unbelievable. Six billion tree seedlings will be imported from Europe. Eventually, the tree-covered area will stretch 950 miles long and average about 10 miles wide. The project will take at least twenty years to complete and will cost about one hundred million dollars a year, or a total of two billion dollars. Each

year one hundred thousand people will work on the project, caring for tree nurseries, planting seedlings, and digging new wells for irrigation canals and reservoirs.

If the project succeeds, by the beginning of the twenty-first century, Algeria will have a new forest covering from seven to eight million acres of land. Imports of wood will no longer be necessary. The high plateaus north of the "Green Belt" can then be reclaimed as agricultural land. And the barren Sahara will be confined.

The "Green Belt" of Algeria may someday be one of the human-constructed wonders of the world.

Coal is mined at Kenadza.

MINERALS

Algeria's mineral reserves were thought to be relatively unimportant for centuries. In the late 1950s, exploration began to show just what riches lay underground.

Large petroleum reserves were discovered in 1956, and a year later production began and pipelines were built to the coast. Twenty years later, Algeria's petroleum reserves were estimated at close to eight billion barrels, and there was hope of finding new deposits.

In 1958, shortly after the first oil was found, a startling and more important deposit came to light. Natural gas deposits were discovered in the same general area —in eastern Algeria near the Tunisian and Libyan borders. The first natural gas was produced in 1961. Further exploration showed that Algeria has a huge share of the world's total reserves of natural gas —at least 10 percent. At present gas reserves are estimated to be four trillion cubic meters, making Algeria fourth in world gas deposits—after the United States, the Soviet Union, and Iran. Some experts believe that further exploration could make Algeria the number-one natural-gas producer in the world.

Other mineral deposits are not large, and their quality is not very good. Iron ore is mined near the Tunisian border and near the spot where Algeria, Morocco, and Spanish Sahara meet. Rich phosphate deposits in the west have almost been depleted, but lower-quality phosphate is being mined in the east. Some coal is mined, but its importance has declined since the discovery of petroleum and natural gas.

Other minerals—many not discovered until after independence and still not fully explored—include lead, zinc, mercury, copper, antimony, tungsten, manganese, and uranium. Most of these deposits are not sizable. But since Algeria's mineral industry is still young, there is hope that someday other mineral deposits as important as those of natural gas will be found.

The People Live in Algeria

POPULATION

The first census in Algeria was taken by the French in 1856. It showed a total population of 2.5 million, of which fewer than 200,000 were Europeans. A little over a century later, in 1960, the total figure had quadrupled to 10.7 million; by then more than one million were Europeans.

After independence, many of the Europeans left Algeria. By the mid-1970s, their total was down to an estimated fifty thousand. But the population growth rate of the Algerians was soaring. In the 1930s it stood at 1.9 percent annually; by 1975 it was up to almost 3.5 percent, and about half the total population was fourteen years of age or younger.

The government has made little effort toward family planning. A few programs to limit population increase have been set up by religious and other private international organizations. President Boumediene has stated officially that the growth rate will decrease automatically as Algeria becomes more developed and the people become better educated. But if this fails to occur, eventually food and employment will become great problems. Algeria's total population was an estimated 16.5 million in 1975. At the present growth rate, it could more than double by the year 2000.

Most of the people live in the thirteen northern wilayas. The two wilayas of the south, in the Sahara, comprise about 90 percent of the nation's area but only about 5 percent of its population. Population density for Algeria as a whole is about eighteen persons per square mile, but in

The faces of these children show the various ethnic groups of Algeria.

The central marketplace in every Algerian town attracts people from every ethnic group and from all walks of life.

the Sahara it is only one per square mile.

More and more, people have been moving to Algeria's towns and cities. During the war for independence, many rural people were displaced or imprisoned or had their homes and villages destroyed. After independence, they moved to the cities to find homes and jobs.

ETHNIC GROUPS

The great majority of Algerians are Arabs and Berbers. Both groups are Muslim and descended from the native Berbers who lived in what is now Algeria twelve hundred years ago.

The Arabs dominate Algeria, making up about 80 percent of the total population. Those in rural areas are apt to have their first loyalty to their individual tribes or villages, rather than to the Algerian nation. The urban Arabs, usually better educated, identify politically with the republic of Algeria. But both groups have close kinship with the people of other Arab nations in North Africa and the Middle East.

The Berbers make up about 20 percent

of the population. They are separated from the Arabs mainly by the language they speak and the fact that they never have intermarried with Arabs. Most of the Berbers live in rural Algeria. There are four main groups, distinguished by the Berber dialect they speak and the part of Algeria in which they live.

Kabyles   The largest Berber group, the Kabyles, live mainly in the eastern portion of the Tell, in the Kabylia and Djurdjura mountains. They are independent people who resisted both the Arab and French conquerors. Even today, they are apt to follow their traditional customs and laws, even if these conflict with the national laws of Algeria.

Chaouias Berbers   This group lives farther east, in the Aures Mountains and along the Tunisian border. The Chaouias Berbers are agricultural people and have not migrated to urban areas, as have the Kabyles. While the Kabyles are joined together by their dialect and ancestry, the Chaouias live separately in villages defined by clans and have little to do with other Chaouias.

M'zabites   These Berbers live in western Algeria, along the southern Moroccan border. They are strict religious Muslims and allow no one but M'zabites to live in their oasis villages.

Tuaregs   Tuaregs are nomadic Berbers of southern Algeria. Many other Tuaregs live farther south in Niger, Mali, and other countries. Before the French arrived, the wandering Tuaregs controlled the Saharan part of Algeria. Today many of them are giving up their nomadic life of sheep- and camel-herding. More and more are working in oil and gas fields in the Sahara and are becoming integrated into Algeria's national life.

RELIGION

Christianity was introduced to Algeria in Roman times. The French conquest brought Roman Catholic churches to the colony; later, Protestant missionaries arrived and attempted to convert the Berbers.

Before independence, few of the one million Europeans in Algeria, mainly Christians, intermarried with Arabs. Most of the Europeans left after independence. Today only about fifty thousand Europeans remain; many of them are professional people residing in Algeria temporarily. There are Roman Catholic and Protestant churches in Algeria's major cities, but the congregations are tiny compared to before independence.

Jewish communities have been important in the Tell region since 1492, when Jews were expelled from Spain. They were granted French citizenship after 1870 and held important positions in business and professional fields. At independence probably 150,000 Jews lived in Algeria. A decade later, however, there were only a few hundred left. By the time the government officially backed the Arabs in the 1967 Arab-Israeli war, most Algerian Jews had moved to France.

For almost twelve hundred years, the

Mauland Kassem was the Minister of Traditional Education and Habus (Religion) in the mid-1970s.

religion of Islam has been the most important moral, social, and cultural basis of Algerian life. For more than a century, the French tried to put down Islamic beliefs and replace them with the tenets of Christianity. But the French were largely unsuccessful. With independence, the importance of Islam in Algeria was renewed. By the mid-1970s, with the exodus of Christians and Jews, more than 99 percent of all Algerians were Muslims.

In 1970 a separate cabinet post, the Ministry of Traditional Education and Habus (Religion), was created to deal with religious shrines and artifacts inherited from the past. As the nation improves its technology and increases its importance in world affairs it will have to deal with many aspects of Islam that conflict with the new culture. It will remain to be seen how the government will deal with that conflict.

CULTURE

One of the main objectives of Algeria's post-independence government has been to replace the European culture introduced by the French with a restoration of the Arabic and Muslim culture of Algeria's past. The Ministry of Information and Culture was created to help the people understand the importance of their arts and traditions.

Most Algerian authors of this century have used French to write in modern literary forms such as novels, short stories, drama, and poetry. As more people learn Arabic, however, there is likely to be a return to classical Arabic poetry and prose.

Since 1968 the National Institute of Music has sought to reintroduce and preserve traditional forms of music, dance, and folklore. The classical Algerian forms of music and dance developed from Arabian styles of the Middle East and Andalusian styles of Spain.

The Algerian National Theater, with stage, radio, and television performances, has introduced the works of modern play-

Folklore groups, like these from Tindouff (above) and Timimoan (below) retell the history of their regions through stories, dance and music.

These artisans transform raw cotton into thread and then into beautiful tapestries which they sell.

wrights who write in Arabic. Theater was brought to Algeria by the French, since the Arab-Islam culture has no tradition of this art form.

Motion pictures produced since independence have won prizes in international cinema festivals. Film production is controlled by the government, and most of the movies made in Algeria are documentaries aimed at educating the public.

Painting has attracted many Algerians ever since the French opened the National School of Fine Arts in Algiers in 1904. Today much of the Algerian painting is of the realistic style and carries themes of revolution and socialism.

During the French occupation, handicrafts thrived only in rural areas. Since 1962, however, the government has opened many handicraft centers throughout Algeria. Today rugs (used on floors or as wall hangings), pottery, and delicate embroidery work are made chiefly in rural areas. In the cities, high-quality ornamental jewelry and brasswork are produced.

The National Library in Algiers had a 700 percent increase in the number of its users in the decade after independence. Special mobile library buses now provide books to the people in rural areas.

HEALTH

Free health care was established after independence under the Social Medical Assistance plan. But it is still not available to all Algerians, for the country does not have enough doctors, nurses, hospitals, and other medical-care facilities. Health standards continue to be very low, partly because the people are ignorant of basic ways to improve their diet and hygiene.

Tuberculosis has been called Algeria's number-one social plague. Although incidence of the disease is low in the Sahara, as many as four out of five persons in the urban areas of the Tell have or once had tuberculosis.

The geographical incidence of trachoma (an eye disease that causes blindness) is reversed—it is greatest in the Sahara. The disease is highly contagious, and nearly everyone there may be afflicted. Trachoma can be cured or at least held in check if treated with a special salve applied to the eyes, but this requires medical treatment that is almost unavailable in the desert.

Malaria epidemics break out everywhere during rainy seasons—from the coast of the Mediterranean to the oases of the Sahara. Other major disease problems include typhus, caused by lack of proper sanitation; typhoid; rabies, which is prevalent among both dogs and wild animals; recurrent fever; and bilharzia, caused by contact with water infected by a certain type of snail. Malnutrition is common among very young children.

Public campaigns of mass vaccination against smallpox, diphtheria, tuberculosis, and tetanus began in 1971. Treatments against trachoma are given to school-age children, who are taught the basic principles of hygiene. The number of hospitals, health centers, and mobile medical facilities is slowly increasing. The training of paramedical personnel (people who can perform some, but not all, medical tasks) will help improve the health of rural people.

Since independence, Algeria has relied on medical assistance (funds, medicine, and personnel) from foreign countries. It will be many years before the republic has enough facilities and personnel to administer an effective health program of its own.

SOCIAL WELFARE

In keeping with its socialistic philosophy, the government considers all health, housing, and social assistance programs as part of its general responsibility for the people's welfare.

A social-security program has been set up for wage earners and their families, but it does not include self-employed farmers and poor residents of the rural areas. Money these workers pay to the program now will be paid back to them after they retire.

The survivors and families of those killed and wounded in the war for independence have been given special pensions. Rehabilitation programs aid the vic-

Social programs, like this modern housing development (left) and clinics for better health care (below), will continue to improve living conditions in Algeria.

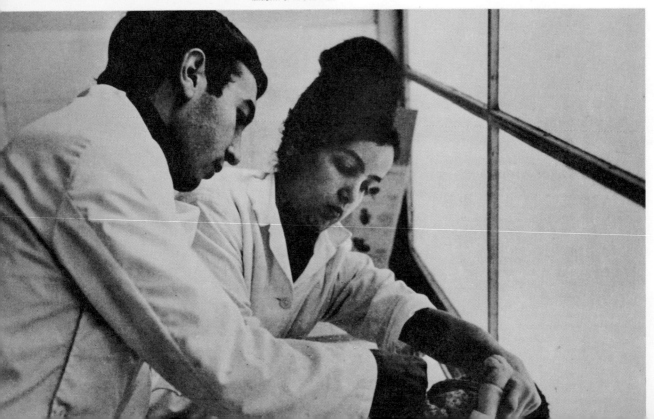

tims of the war, those afflicted with serious diseases, and handicapped and orphaned children. Youth centers specialize not only in recreational activities but also teach basic reading, writing, and mathematics to those who have never attended school.

All of these social programs are presently available only to those who live in cities and towns. Until Algeria's economy improves, social welfare will not spread to the unemployed, to those who live in small villages, or to the people of the Sahara.

HOUSING

During and after the war for independence, four factors caused a serious lack of housing in Algeria. First, many dwellings were bombed and destroyed in the cities. Second, up to two million rural people were put in prisons or detention camps and their villages destroyed. Third, after the war, many of those displaced persons moved to urban areas, which soon became overcrowded. And last, and most important, Algeria's population increased dramatically between 1960 and 1975.

Some thirty-four thousand housing units were completed or started during a three-year program for housing from 1967 to 1969. As part of the Four-Year Plan for economic development announced in 1970, eighty thousand more housing units were to be built. Most of these were government-owned public housing.

But even all these new units will not be enough. It became obvious near the end of the Four-Year Plan that the government alone could not build enough housing for Algeria's rapidly growing population. Until a private construction industry is developed, the lack of adequate housing will continue to be a pressing problem.

The People Work in Algeria

AGRICULTURE

Although Algeria is well on its way toward becoming an industrialized nation, most Algerians still earn their living through farming. About two-thirds of the working people work in agriculture, although this industry contributes only about one-third of the nation's total income.

Crops can be grown only on about 10 percent of Algeria's total area. The farming lands are scattered through the Tell region in the north and, to a lesser extent, through parts of the high plateaus where there is enough rainfall.

The most important permanent, or year-round, crops are grapes and citrus fruits. The French introduced grape vineyards to Algeria in the mid-nineteenth century when a disease caused by insects destroyed French vineyards. Since the Islam religion forbids the drinking of alcoholic beverages most Algerian wine has been—and still is—sold abroad, mainly in France, where it often is mixed with French wine before being sold.

Citrus fruits grown in Algeria include oranges, tangerines, lemons, and grapefruit. Other tree crops are olives, figs, and dates. Dates are the only crop grown in the Sahara, where thousands of date palms can thrive around the larger oases.

About one-third of Algeria's farmland is planted with cereal crops—primarily wheat, barley, oats, corn, and rice. The major vegetable crops are potatoes, tomatoes, and green beans. Some cotton and

Since Western farm machinery, like this combine, has come to Algeria, harvesting wheat has been done much more efficiently.

tobacco are also grown on this land.

Livestock is raised north of the Sahara and makes up perhaps one-fourth of the total agricultural production. Climate and rainfall are so unpredictable there that nomads must drive their livestock herds from place to place to find adequate drinking water and pasture.

In 1972 the total livestock population included more than seven million sheep, more than two million goats, slightly fewer than one million cattle, and fewer than one million horses, mules, donkeys, and camels combined.

LAND OWNERSHIP

After the French took over Algeria in 1830, they seized much of the land—including that used for agriculture. The land they seized included private property, tribal lands, land that had been donated to Islamic religious groups, and land that had been held for over one thousand years by the different governments that ruled what is now Algeria.

By the time of independence, only about one-tenth of Algeria's agricultural land was owned by Algerians. Most privately owned farms were small—about twenty-five acres—and supported large families or family groups.

When the French left in 1962, the new Algerian government took ownership of all the farmlands once owned by Europeans. A socialized system of ownership called *autogestion* was set up, whereby the government owned the farms but they were run by workers' management teams. By 1970, 80 percent of the total agricultural land—including croplands and livestock grazing lands—was operated in this socialistic method of farming.

The Agrarian Revolution began in 1971. Large farms were divided into smaller plots; tools, seeds, and fertilizers were distributed to the management teams; and general education regarding reclamation and irrigation of the land was given to the farmers.

Through modern farming practices, the government hopes to increase crop yields and make effective use of land that has been lying unused for years. Irrigation and flood-control measures have changed many useless acres into suitable farmland. New machinery and modern agricultural techniques are being introduced. Little by little, Algerian farmers are learning the modern ways of agriculture.

INDUSTRY

Like agriculture, industry underwent a change from private European ownership to socialistic worker-management control after independence. Through autogestion, the government controlled and ran almost

Workers harvest citrus fruits (opposite top) and grapes (opposite bottom), two of Algeria's most important agricultural products.

This liquefication plant at Arzew converts natural gas to a liquid form so it can be more easily transported to ports in England and France.

all of Algeria's industrial and manufacturing facilities, especially the most important—those involving minerals.

Oil production in the early 1970s was more than one million barrels a day, and natural gas production rose to nearly four billion cubic meters a year. Natural gas production will increase even more as more pipelines are built from the eastern gas fields to the coast.

Soon after independence, most foreign oil and gas firms in Algeria were nationalized. A government agency called Sonatrach was formed to operate the oil and gas fields, build pipelines, and sell the products to foreign nations.

Because Algerians did not have the technical or financial capabilities to do all the mineral exploration and refining, some concessions were granted to foreign firms. However, Sonatrach retained a 51 percent interest in all of these foreign concessions. By 1973 Sonatrach was the ninth-largest oil-producing firm in the world, and production of natural gas in Algeria still continues to increase.

Although oil reserves may eventually be depleted, natural gas reserves are so huge that, for the foreseeable future, these two minerals will be of prime importance in making Algeria an industrialized, self-sufficient nation. At present these two minerals bring in at least three-fourths of Algeria's income.

Other mineral industries include iron and steel mills at Annaba, and mercury, zinc, lead, and kaolin factories. The mining of phosphate rock was once Algeria's main mineral industry—before the discovery of oil and gas. Although the quality and quantity of remaining phosphate deposits have decreased, Algeria still produces a large amount of phosphate rock. In 1974 Algeria joined with the other major world suppliers of phosphate rock in increasing prices by at least 400 percent.

All solid mineral research, exploitation, and production in Algeria is under the control of the governmental agency Sonarem. This agency is similar to Sonatrach, which controls oil and gas.

The production of electricity is controlled by the national power and gas company, called Sonelgaz. As industry grows in Algeria, more electricity will be needed to run the factories and mills. Dams have been constructed to create electricity by hydroelectric methods; natural gas and diesel fuel are also used in its production. In the decade after independence, electrical output doubled.

Food processing, including canning, remains the largest nonmineral industry. Food-processing companies and most other manufacturing companies have been nationalized by the government. Tractors, motors, motorcycles, and industrial vehicles are made at a plant in Constantine. There are several factories producing cement, brick, glass, tile, and other construction materials.

The government agency called Sonitex

A steel-manufacturing complex at Annaba produces the raw materials for many of Algeria's other industries.

MINISTRY OF INFORMATION

controls the textile mills, almost all of which came into existence after 1962. Tanneries, many using goatskin and sheepskin, produce the leather used in new plants where shoes, sandals, handbags, and leather clothing are made. Five factories produce soap products and oils.

TRADE AND BUSINESS

As a French colony, Algeria was forced to conduct most of its trade with France. Even when political ties to France were cut in 1962, that tradition continued. Today France supplies about one-third of Algeria's imports and buys about one-fourth of its exports. Trade with France is declining, however, as Algeria is seeking more distant trading partners, including the United States, the USSR, and other Communist-bloc countries.

Algeria has obtained financial loans and technical assistance from many countries, including France, the USSR, the United States, and Japan.

After France, Algeria's major foreign trade (both imports and exports) is with West Germany, Italy, Spain, and other North African countries.

Algeria's major exports are petroleum (from 70 to 80 percent of total exports in recent years), wine, natural gas, citrus fruits, and minerals. Major imports are foods, including cereal grains; manufactured goods used both in industry and for consumer use; and agricultural and transportation equipment.

In the mid-1960s, Algeria's exports exceeded its imports, giving the country a positive balance of trade—that is, more money was received for exports than was spent for imports. At the beginning of the 1970s, however, this trend was reversed, for Algeria imported a lot of industrial machinery and equipment. The rapidly expanding production and sale of natural gas, however, should once again give Algeria a positive balance of trade.

In 1963 the Central Bank of Algeria was established to replace the French-founded Bank of Algeria. At the same time, a new national currency was introduced to replace the Algerian franc, which had been equal in value to the French franc. The new currency, completely independent of other moneys, is called the *dinar*. It is divided into hundredths, like the American dollar.

THE LABOR FORCE

Unemployment became a major problem immediately after independence. Many of the French who left Algeria were skilled workers or technicians. Since there were no trained Algerians to replace them, many factories and businesses closed. Unemployment was made worse by the rapid population rise and the migration of unskilled workers to the cities and towns.

Aside from the two-thirds of the work force who work in agriculture, the government is the largest employer in Algeria, since it has nationalized so many of the formerly French-owned large businesses and industries.

Relatively few women hold regular wage-earning jobs, but many women work on the farms.

Algerian men began emigrating to France to find work since World War I, when they replaced Frenchmen who were serving in the French army. Under the Evian Agreement of 1962, which gave Algeria the right to become independent, this migration for employment purposes was allowed to continue. Later, however, migration quotas were set up.

In 1974 the total number of Algerians living in France was estimated at anywhere from 350,000 to 850,000—most of them men, but some dependent women and children. In the early 1970s, many French citizens began to protest against Algerians working in France, arguing that they took up housing and jobs needed by the French. Some of the protest was said to be based on racism, and there were incidents of attacks and demonstrations against the Algerian Arabs.

The Algerian government hopes that eventually it will be able to provide jobs at home for all of its workers now in France. But such a policy cannot be put into effect yet because of the widespread unemployment in Algeria.

TRANSPORTATION

Algeria's industrial revolution will not succeed totally until adequate means of

UNITED NATIONS

Classes that teach keypunching and other skills help women to enter Algeria's job market. Traditionally, only men worked away from the home, but this is changing.

transportation exist to move raw materials, equipment, and finished goods, as well as passengers, from place to place.

The first railroads were built by the French in the late 1800s. Except for a few branch lines laid to new industrial zones since 1962, they remain the only railroads in use today.

Standard-gauge lines run parallel to the coast of Algeria, connecting the nation with the neighboring countries of Morocco and Tunisia, and extending northward to the main ports, including Algiers, Oran, and Constantine. There are five narrow-

gauge lines extending southward from the Tell region into the high plateaus. No railroad lines cross the Sahara.

In 1975 there were approximately twenty-five hundred miles of rail lines, all run by the National Society of Algerian Railways. Both freight and passenger traffic doubled in the decade after independence.

The best and most important roads in Algeria also run between the coastal cities. In 1972 there were about fifty thousand miles of roadways. About one-quarter of the total was paved highways (mainly in the north along the coast), one-quarter was semi-improved roads leading south, and one-half was unimproved rural trails and lanes.

Following the practice of the rest of the world, the Algerian government is concentrating on improving old roads and building new ones, rather than extending its railway system. From 1966 to 1969 alone, seventy-three million dollars was spent in road maintenance and improvement. In recent years, roads have been constructed to the new oil and natural gas fields in eastern Algeria.

Roads in the Sahara are difficult to build and almost impossible to maintain. They are constantly buried by blowing sand, even where windbreaks (or, more accurately, sand breaks) are built alongside of them.

Despite these hazards, in 1971 the government began construction of a one-thousand-mile-long Trans-Saharan Road to run southward from the town of El Golea, in central Algeria, to the border with Niger. Once completed, it should greatly increase and simplify trade with the nations of central Africa. To encourage tourist traffic, motels, restaurants, and service stations will be built along the roadway.

Air traffic in and out of Algeria is dominated by the government-controlled airline, Air Algeria. It operates international flights to the major cities of North Africa and to many European capitals. Domestic flights reach most of the larger cities and towns of Algeria, including some large oasis towns.

There are about two dozen main airports, half of which can handle large planes. The major international airports are at Oran, Constantine, Annaba, and Algiers. The airport at Algiers has runways accommodating large jets, and it handles most of the country's freight and passenger traffic.

Another government airline, the Air Travel Society (STA), has smaller planes that fly freight and passengers to small airports in the interior.

COMMUNICATIONS

Algeria's communications media are also owned and operated by the government. The Algerian Press Service is a na-

Opposite: The construction of new roads (top left), modern railroads (top right), and airports (bottom) make travel easier inside and into Algeria.

tional news agency that furnishes both Algerian and international news to radio, television, and newspapers.

There are four daily newspapers in Algeria—two published in French and two in Arabic. Their total circulation is about two hundred thousand. In addition, about two or three times as many weekly newspapers and periodicals are published.

While the press has a certain amount of freedom, it is not allowed to criticize the basic policies of the government. Foreign publications are usually available, but often they are banned if they criticize governmental policies.

The Algerian Radio and Television System came into being in 1962, when the French-owned audiovisual company was nationalized. Since then new studios and transmitters have been built that can send radio and TV programs throughout the country. In 1972 there were about 750,000 radios in Algeria and about 250,000 TV sets.

Both radio and TV also send out, in French and Arabic, general educational and documentary programs aimed at increasing the people's knowledge of Arabic history and culture and the socialistic principles of the government.

Since independence, the government has spent millions of dinars in improving and increasing telephone and telegraph services. In the early 1970s, there were about two hundred thousand telephones in use in Algeria, most of them in the north.

Enchantment of Algeria

RIPE FOR TOURISM

Algeria is situated geographically in a perfect spot to attract tourists. It lies at the crossroads of three different worlds—the Mediterranean world of Europe and North Africa, the religious world of the Muslims, and the ethnic world of black Africa to the south.

Within Algeria's borders, there are winter resorts on snow-covered mountains, seaside beaches and bays with breathtaking sites for water sports, and fascinating palm-shaded oasis towns in the midst of a great desert. Geographically and physically, Algeria is varied and exciting.

Until the present day, the international travel world has not been attracted to Algeria. Under the French, tourism was slight. Only a few Frenchmen and other southern Europeans visited its coastal cit-ies. During the long war for independence, few travelers dared to visit the colony. Once independence was achieved, problems of housing, farming, unemployment, the economy, and other urgent requirements for building a new nation left little time or money to popularize Algeria's beauty and fascination.

In 1966 the government adopted a Charter of Tourism as part of the general industrial revolution. The government realized that a tourist industry would help Algeria's economic development. Hotels and resort spas were built, with new roads leading to them. The Institute for Hotel and Tourist Studies created training facilities for tourist guides, hotel employees, and travel-agency personnel.

It became clear that Algeria's historical and religious heritage could become a prime attraction to the rest of the world.

The sites of ancient Carthaginian and Roman ruins and centuries-old Muslim mosques were uncovered and rehabilitated. Museums displaying archaeological, ethnic, and religious treasures were built, enlarged, and improved.

During the last quarter of the twentieth century, Algeria may become one of the most diversive tourist stops in the world. By accenting its past and by bringing its present up to modern-day status, Algeria will have a bright future as a holiday and vacation center.

ALGIERS

Algiers is the capital city, largest city, main port, and most likely the oldest city in Algeria. First settled by the Phoenicians about three thousand years ago, succeeding centuries have seen occupation by Romans, Vandals, Byzantines, Arabs, Spaniards, Mediterranean traders, and finally the French.

Some signs of these long and varied occupations are still visible today. There are Roman Catholic cathedrals built by the French, houses built and lived in by pirates, and elaborately designed Arabian mosques. Ancient Roman cemeteries have been uncovered during excavations for modern buildings.

Just offshore in the city's bay are a number of tiny islands. The main island was captured by the Spanish in the sixteenth century; the Spanish dominated Algiers from it, although they never took the city itself. Today a large bridge or causeway leads from the city to this island. The other small islands disappeared long ago, hidden under the piers and jetties protruding from the mainland that help form the great port.

Algiers has long been known as the "White City." From the sea, it presents a spectacular sight, rising in a semicircle around the bay, climbing a sharply inclined hill that reaches about eight hundred feet. Its whitewashed buildings and green trees and parks are reflected in the incredible blue of the Mediterranean. Recently, tall modern buildings—apartments, business centers, and hotels—have risen above the old white houses and shops.

In general, the business district of the city lies in the narrow space between the harbor facilities of the bay and the hill behind. About halfway up the hillside is the famous Casbah, built in the 1500s by the Turks and used as a residence by the deys. *Casbah* is an Arabic word meaning "walled citadel" or "fortress," which is exactly what the Casbah once was. Later, under the French, it became the part of the city where the native Algerians lived. Today many Mediterranean cities have casbahs, or native quarters, but the Casbah of Algiers remains the most famous.

Narrow streets cut like the walkways of a maze through the Casbah's old and

Roman ruins, like this archway to an ancient city at Timgad, show the beauty and long history of Algeria.

Against a backdrop of skyscrapers lies the Casbah (old quarter), the first section of Algiers that was settled. Today it is a section noted for local color and excitement.

sometimes crumbling white houses and shops. Overhead, balconies seem to reach out to touch the buildings across the way. Mosques and marketplaces exist side by side. Thousands of persons, natives and tourists alike, crowd through the streets, buying and selling in a bright, colorful jumble of sight and sound.

During the war for independence, the Casbah was a center of anti-French sentiment and activities. Much of the time it was barricaded from the rest of the city, and natives could enter and leave only by showing identification papers. Soon after

independence, the new government expressed a desire to declare the Casbah a historic site and move its residents to new housing at the edge of Algiers. A tremendous public outcry soon put an end to those plans. The Casbah today continues to exist as an unofficial historic site—but a lively, active one, not a quiet museumlike ruin.

High above the Casbah, at the top of the city's hill, are new apartment buildings and expensive villas surrounded by trees and gardens. A new hotel looks out over the bay, and there are shopping centers

84

and a stadium that seats eighty thousand people.

Some of the other enchanting sights and sites of Algiers include the Experimental Garden near the stadium, a quiet refuge of trees, flowers, and fountains, with a museum of antiquities; the Bardo Palace from Turkish times, now a museum of ethnology; the National Library, with shelf space for more than two million books; the University of Algiers; and the many governmental buildings, some of which were once palace-homes for the leaders of the foreign nations that occupied Algiers.

ORAN AND CONSTANTINE

Algiers is located about midway along the Algerian coastline. The country's second- and third-largest cities are set almost equally as far to the east and west of the capital:

Oran lies to the west, not far from the Moroccan border. It has been called the most spectacular of Algeria's cities. Oran sits on a high plateau that ends in cliffs plunging down to the Mediterranean and Oran's port, which is smaller but more modern than Algiers's. Behind the city are rugged, rocky mountains rising to fifteen hundred feet. They seem to close in on the city, keeping it a compact entity squeezed between peaks and the sea. Like Algiers, Oran's architecture is a blend of antique and modern—old buildings including mosques and a casbah from the days of Turkey and France, along with modern of-

SHIFTING SANDS OF ALGERIA

This narrow span crosses high above the Gorge of Constantine.

fice buildings and apartment houses.

Algeria's third-largest city, Constantine, lies to the east of Algiers, near the border with Tunisia. Not a port city, it lies about fifty miles from the Mediterranean on the banks of the Rhumel River, which cuts a deep gorge through the center of the city. Constantine was founded by the Carthaginians and became the capital, called Cirta, of the Roman kingdom of Numidia. It was destroyed in 311 A.D. during the Berber revolt against the Romans and later was rebuilt by the Emperor Constantine I,

Algeria is a land where past and present meet. The ancient Roman ruins (opposite left) and the irrigation ditch through the timeless sands of the Sahara (opposite right) provide a sharp contrast with the modern University of Algiers (above) and the city's busy port (below).

from whom it took its present name. Today, as for centuries past, Constantine is the crossroads for trade and culture in eastern Algeria.

BEACHES, SPAS, AND MOUNTAINS

The blue waters and bays of the Mediterranean lap against sandy beaches in some spots along the Algerian coastline and splash against brightly colored rocky cliffs in others. Since 1966 the government has chosen some of the most beautiful seaside sites for a chain of resorts. Lavish hotels have been built, with pools, patios, tennis courts, restaurants, and nightclubs. Small private bungalows and more expensive villas look down on the sea.

To the west of Algiers are Moretti, with a beach claimed to be one of the finest in the world; Zeralda, whose beach is called Golden Sands and is surrounded by outbreaks of red rocks and a pine forest; and Tipasa, with Roman and Carthaginian ruins which make it one of the finest archaeological sites along the Mediterranean. Fifteen miles from Algiers white and tan buildings of a suburb stretch out into the bay, providing a magnificent sailboat marina. Oran's chief resort is The Andalouses, also known for its Roman ruins.

East of Algiers, in the Constantine area, are the port of Bedjaia, known for its nearby colony of wild Barbary apes, and the town of Skikda, long the seaside vacation spot for the residents of Constantine.

The mineral-spring spas of Algeria were famous even in Roman times. Ever since then, people have visited the spas regularly to drink and bathe in their curative waters. Many people claim that the sulfated and bicarbonated waters bring relief from such ailments as rheumatism, arthritis, and various other illnesses.

The government has declared five of the mineral springs to be national health resorts, and a program of building hotels, bungalows, and swimming facilities is well underway. The five national spas and other regional spas are all located in the Tell region, not far from the coast.

It seems odd that a nation that is mainly desert can have winter-sports resorts, but such is the case with Algeria. At many places in the two ranges of the Atlas Mountains, snow covers the highest peaks in winter, and skiing is a popular sport. Only forty miles south of Algiers, two ski lifts have been built through a magnificent cedar forest. Another winter resort is at Ain el Hamman in the Kabylia Mountains. In summer the mountain resort facilities are used as headquarters for camping, hiking, and fishing.

THE SAHARA

Algeria's largest natural feature may someday turn out to be its most important tourist attraction. For centuries the seemingly endless Sahara in southern Algeria was crossed only by camel caravans. With the completion of the north-south Trans-

Saharan Road, however, travelers will be able to follow in the wake of the caravans—riding leisurely in cars and resting comfortably at oasis resorts complete with modern hotels, swimming pools, and shops. At some spots, less-lavish inns called *caravanserais* cater to less-affluent travelers.

Handicraft centers have been created at some of the larger desert towns, giving tourists an opportunity to observe the making of intricately carved jewelry and woodwork, leatherwork, and rainbow-colored rugs and textiles. Algeria's handicrafts are an important inheritance of the nation's past. But in the first half of the twentieth century, they were on the point of dying out, forgotten and ignored by the French. Today the future of handicrafts is tied to the future of tourism in Algeria. As the tourist trade develops, it is hoped that visitors will buy the exotic handmade works of art, spread word of them throughout the world, and create an international market for them.

As exciting as is Algeria's present and as hopeful its future, it will be the past that truly brings the people of this republic together. The production of oil and natural gas will aid the economy and make possible improvements in health, education, and housing. Only when the people realize, however, that despite thousands of years of occupation by foreigners there still exists a culture that is specifically Algerian will a true spirit of nationalism arise.

Algeria's heritage is not only Roman and Carthaginian ruins, not only mosques built by Turkish invaders, not only the bitter memories of a century and a half of French rule. It is also mountains, beaches, spas, and deserts that existed long before the first Phoenicians set up trading posts on the coast. It is yellow and orange frescoes painted on caves in the Ahaggar Mountains many thousands of years ago.

Most of all, the heritage of today's Algerians is the knowledge that the invaders came and the invaders went, but the people of Algeria remained. And since 1962, they have been independent—free of all foreign dominance, good or bad. The earliest Berber tribesmen, free to wander where their fancy took them, have much in common with their descendants—the Algerians of today.

Handy Reference Section

INSTANT FACTS

Political:

Official Name—Democratic and Popular Republic of Algeria

Capital—Algiers

Form of Government—Socialistic republic

Monetary Unit—Dinar

Official Language—Arabic

Official Religion—Islam

Flag—Green and white background (left half, green; right half, white), on which is superimposed a red crescent on the left and a red star within the points of the crescent.

Geographical:

Area—919,590 square miles

Highest Point—Mt. Tahat, in Ahaggar Mountains (about 10,000 feet)

Lowest Point—Sea level

Greatest Width (east to west)—1200 miles

Greatest Length (north to south)—1100 miles

POPULATION

Total Population—16,500,000 (1975 estimate)

Population Density—18 persons per square mile

Population Profile—about 80 percent Arabs; about 20 percent Berbers; fewer than 1 percent Europeans

Literacy Rate—25 to 30 percent

GOVERNMENTAL DIVISIONS

Wilayas	*Capital cities*
Algiers	Algiers
Annaba	Annaba
Aures (Batna)	Batna

Constantine	Constantine	Saida	Saida
El-Asnam	Orleansville	Saoura (Sahara)	Bechar
Medea (Titteri)	Medea	Setif	Setif
Mostaganem	Mostaganem	Tiaret	Tiaret
Oasis	Ouargla	Tizi-Ouzou	Tizi-Ouzou
Oran	Oran	Tlemcen	Tlemcen

YOU HAVE A DATE WITH HISTORY

1200 B.C.—Phoenicians found trading posts along northern Africa coast

201 B.C.—Massinissa battles Carthaginians at Zama, is given Numidia by Romans

313 A.D.—Christianity becomes official religion of Eastern Roman empire, including present-day Algeria

439—Vandals conquer North Africa

534—Byzantines drive Vandals from North Âfrica

700—Berber tribesmen of Algeria conquered by Muslims

800—Berbers expel Muslims, begin seven hundred years of civil wars

1500—Spain controls Algiers by occupying Penon Island in Bay of Algiers

1518—Turks begin 300-year domination of Algeria

1815—U.S. naval captain Stephen Decatur ends tribute-taking by pirates

1830—French capture Algiers

1834—French declare North African coast a French colony

1847—End of Muslim Algerian holy war against French; European emigration to Algeria begins

1871—Most serious anti-French rebellion by Berbers occurs

1909—University of Algiers founded

1914—French completely occupy all of Saharan region of Algeria

1926—First anticolonialism group founded by Messali Hadj

1937—Anti-French Algerian People's Party formed

1942—Allied forces liberate Algeria from German-backed Vichy government

1945—Riot breaks out in Setif at end of World War II (May 8)

1947—Charles DeGaulle insists that Algeria remain a French colony

1954—National Liberation Front and National Liberation Army begin guerilla war for independence (November 1)

1956—Battle of Algiers begins (December); large oil reserves discovered

1957—Battle of Algiers ends (September)

1958—Natural gas deposits discovered

1959—DeGaulle offers Algeria promise of independence

1960—*Colons* begin extremist campaign against Algerians (January)

1961—FLN leaders meet with French

government officials in France to try to bring about peace

1962—Cease-fire signed in Evian, France (March 18); Algerians vote for independence (July 1); Algeria declared independent (July 3); Houari Boumediene takes power in coup (September 9); Ahmed Ben Bella elected premier

1963—Constitution adopted (September); Algeria helps found Organization of African Unity (OAU) (April)

1965—Ben Bella ousted by coup (June 19), Boumediene takes power, constitution suspended

1968—Government begins to nationalize all foreign-owned companies

1969—Wilaya Code decreed

1970—Four-Year Plan announced

1971—Agrarian Revolution announced; Trans-Saharan Road begun

1973—Algeria joins other oil-producing nations in raising prices and embargoes; conference of Arab nations meet in Algiers (November); fourth Summit Conference of Non-Aligned Countries meets in Algiers

1974—Boumediene addresses United Nations; four-year Industrial Revolution starts; last important manufacturing firms nationalized; foreign minister Abdel-Aziz Bouteflika elected president of UN General Assembly (September)

1975—First trees of "Green Belt" to hold back Sahara planted

Index

About the Author

With the publication of his first book for school use when he was twenty, **Allan Carpenter** began a career as an author that has spanned more than 135 books—with more still to be published in the Enchantment of Africa series for Childrens Press. After teaching in the public schools of Des Moines, Mr. Carpenter began his career as an educational publisher at the age of twenty-one when he founded the magazine *Teachers Digest*. In the field of educational periodicals, he was responsible for many innovations. During his many years in publishing, he has perfected a highly organized approach to handling large volumes of factual material: after extensive traveling and having collected all possible materials, he systematically reviews and organizes everything. From his apartment high in Chicago's John Hancock Building, Allan recalls: "My collection and assimilation of materials on the states and countries began before the publication of my first book." Allan is the founder of Carpenter Publishing House and of Infordata International, Inc., publishers of *Issues in Education* and *Index to U.S. Government Periodicals*. When he is not writing or traveling, his principal avocation is music. He has been the principal bassist of many symphonies, and he managed the country's leading non-professional symphony for twenty-five years.